Weird but true!

know-it-all

The Middle Ages

MICHAEL BURGAN

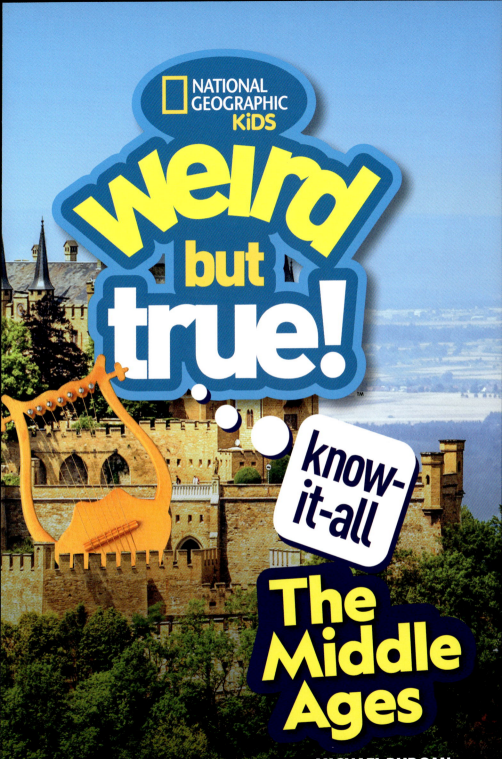

NATIONAL GEOGRAPHIC KiDS
Weird but true!
know-it-all
The Middle Ages

MICHAEL BURGAN
Illustrated by Carmen Sanchez

National Geographic
Washington, D.C.

CONTENTS

WELCOME TO THE MIDDLE AGES! 6
ARE YOU A MIDDLE AGES ACE? 8
THE ROMAN EMPIRE 10
END OF AN EMPIRE 12
GO EAST, YOUNG ROMAN 14
SPOTLIGHT: MONASTIC LIFE 16
HOW TO CREATE AN ILLUSTRATED MANUSCRIPT 18
THE POWER COUPLE OF THE EAST 20
A COMPETING EMPIRE 24
SPOTLIGHT: THE SILK ROAD 26
THE PROPHET FOR A NEW RELIGION 28
THE RISE OF ISLAM 30
A NEW WESTERN POWER 32
CHARLEMAGNE AND THE SPREAD OF CHRISTIANITY 34
SPOTLIGHT: FARMING 38
VICTORIOUS VIKINGS 40
THE VIKING WORLD 42
BURY INTERESTING GRAVES 44
MY, MY, MAYA 46
THE WONDERS OF CHICHÉN ITZÁ 48
MAJOR MOUNDS 50
SPOTLIGHT: IN THE MOOD FOR FOOD 52
LIFE IN THE DESERT 54
THE LAND OF GOLD 56
FIND YOUR PLACE IN MEDIEVAL EUROPE 58
KNOW YOUR SOCIAL RANKS 60
SHOGUNS AND SAMURAI 62
THE SAMURIGHT STUFF 64
AN INDIAN EMPIRE 66
RAH RAH FOR RAJARAJA 68
STRONG SONG 70
SPOTLIGHT: SONG SMARTS 72
A WORLD OF BELIEFS 74
THE CRUSADES 76
CRUSADERS IN CONTROL 78
WHAT TO WEAR TO WAR 80
A CRUSADING FAMILY 82
SPECIAL ORDERS 84
SPOTLIGHT: SACRED SITES 86
INSIDE AND OUTSIDE NOTRE DAME 88
KNOW YOUR MEDIEVAL WARFARE 90
DEFENDER OF ISLAM 92
ISLAM'S IMPACT 94

SPOTLIGHT: GREAT MUSLIM THINKERS	96
BARONS VERSUS A KING	98
TOURNAMENT TIME	100
A KHAN-FIDENT RULER	102
ONE BECOMES FOUR	104
GREATEST OF THE GREAT	106
SPOTLIGHT: A LOOK AT BOOKS	108
SECOND TO NUN	110
SCHOOL'S IN	112
LET'S EAT!	114
HOUSIN' AROUND	116
CLOTHES MINDED	118
HOW TO BE A MEDIEVAL KID	120
CITY LIFE IN WESTERN EUROPE	122
THE DEADLIEST DISEASE	124
DEALING WITH DEATH	126
KNOW YOUR HOME REMEDIES	128
SPOTLIGHT: WORKIN' FOR A LIVING	130
NOBODY'S FOOL	132
DO THE RIGHT THING	134
SPOTLIGHT: LEGENDS AND LORE	136
EXPLORE A MEDIEVAL CASTLE	138
WHO LIVED WHERE	140
A GREAT GOLDEN KINGDOM	142
MADE IN THE TRADE	144
A TRIP TO THE FAIR	146
HOW TO TELL TIME	148
ALL ABOUT THE AZTEC	150
AN INCA-REDIBLE EMPIRE	152
SPOTLIGHT: THE HEART OF ART	154
WAR WITHOUT END	156
JOAN JUMPS IN	158
SPOTLIGHT: DO THE CRIME, DO THE TIME	160
SPOTLIGHT: MYTHS, MAGIC, AND MONSTERS	162
TALE ME MORE	164
SPOTLIGHT: MAKING BEAUTIFUL MUSIC	166
A TURKISH EMPIRE	168
THE WORLD AT THE END OF THE MIDDLE AGES	170
A NEW AGE	172
GLOSSARY	174
INTERVIEW: PETER BROWN	178
TEST YOUR KNOWLEDGE	180
INDEX	182
PHOTO CREDITS	189
CREDITS	192

WELCOME TO THE MIDDLE AGES!

Jousting knights entertaining kings and queens. Castles with thick walls, guarded by soldiers with swords and spears. Peasants sweating in the fields while wealthy lords and ladies dine in beautiful palaces. Vikings coming ashore from swift ships to raid villages.

You might be familiar with these images from books, movies, plays, or television shows. What do they have in common? They all come from a time period known as the Middle Ages, or medieval times. You may have also heard this period called "the Dark Ages," but it wasn't because folks didn't have electric lights (or even matchsticks). Rather this is a way of saying the period was marked by violence (including wars and deadly rivalries over land and religion), as well as a lack of records of historical events.

A good bit of fighting *did* go on during the Middle Ages, no question. But there was great learning as well. Religions of all kinds played an important role in many people's lives. The era also saw the creation of inventions that are still around today. Ever found your way with a compass or bought something with paper money? Then you've used something that first appeared during the Middle Ages.

MIDDLE OF WHAT?

But when exactly did the Middle Ages begin and end? And what were they in the middle of, anyway? The Middle Ages lasted for about 1,000 years, from about 476 C.E. to around 1500. This period started after the end of the Roman Empire (27 B.C.E. to 476 C.E.), which began in—surprise!—Rome. Roman leaders and their troops then spread Roman rule to include large parts of Europe and chunks of North Africa and Asia. Near the end of the Middle Ages began a period known as the Renaissance (about 1300 to 1600). It featured a burst of great art and writing. Like the Roman Empire, the Renaissance began in Italy before spreading across Europe.

A GLOBAL AGE

The images of the Middle Ages described earlier come mostly from Europe. But amazing things were happening all over the world during this period. The Middle Ages saw the rise of great empires around the globe. In this book, you'll go from North America to China to Africa and all points in between—and you won't even need a passport!

So, get ready—you're about to charge straight into the Middle Ages!

WHAT'S IN A WORD?

Medieval

There was nothing evil about medieval times. The word "medieval" comes from Latin words that mean "middle age," so it's just a fancy way of saying the same thing. The word was first used in the early 1800s. People today sometimes use it to call something old-fashioned—as if it came from the Middle Ages.

MARKING TIME

What's up with all the letters you see next to the years here? They're part of the way historians, and others, mark time—using the birth of Jesus Christ as Year 1 of the "common era," or C.E. The years before Year 1 are noted as B.C.E., meaning "before the common era." For B.C.E. dates, years count down to Year 1, so 1000 B.C.E. is 999 years before 1 B.C.E. And 1 B.C.E. is the last year of that era. The next year is 1 C.E., and the years go up after that. So, 1000 C.E. is 999 years after 1 C.E. In addition, the number of the century is the number of centuries that have occurred since 1 C.E. For example, the 100s were the second century to occur in the era, and the 2000s are the 21st century. And when you see "ca." or "c." before a date, that means circa, or about that date, because the exact date is not known.

Are you a MIDDLE AGES ACE?

Before you step back in time to the Middle Ages, let's see how much you already know about the people and places of this era. Try your hand at a little True-or-False quiz. Don't worry, you won't be graded—it's just for fun.

In medieval times, everyone thought the world was flat. It took Christopher Columbus's voyage in 1492 to prove the world was round.

FALSE!

Some Middle Ages folks may have wondered if the world was flat, but great thinkers of ancient times wrote that Earth was like a giant ball in space. And educated people in the Middle Ages thought so, too. But it is true that European medieval mapmakers didn't know exactly what the rest of the world looked like—or that the Americas, Australia, and Antarctica even existed!

Sow unfair.

Animals in the Middle Ages could be arrested and executed if they hurt humans.

TRUE!

Animals such as dogs and pigs could be arrested and brought to court if they hurt people or destroyed property.

In 1000 C.E., London was the world's largest city.

FALSE!

With a population of about nine million today, London is one big city. But in medieval times, it was just a tiny town compared to Kaifeng, China. In the year 1000, one million people lived in Kaifeng.

Ivar the Boneless, Harald Bluetooth, and Alfonso the Slobberer were all European warriors or rulers during medieval times.

TRUE!

Nicknames come in all flavors—they can be funny or cruel or describe a person's looks. Many medieval rulers ended up with nicknames, though today we may not know exactly where those nicknames came from.

Ivar the Boneless was a Viking warrior, who in 865 led a raid on England and captured chunks of land there. He wasn't really boneless, of course—otherwise he couldn't have picked up a sword! But some stories say he had a bone disease and had to be carried into battle.

Harald Bluetooth was a 10th-century Danish king who spread Christianity in his land. Some historians say a bad tooth—one that was actually black, not blue—led to his nickname. Many centuries later, in honor of Harald, Bluetooth was chosen as the name for a wireless system used by smartphones and computers.

Starting at the end of the 12th century, Alfonso IX ruled the kingdoms of Leon and Galicia, in what is today Spain. He earned the Spanish nickname *baboso,* which can mean "slobberer" in English. It was said that Alfonso foamed at the mouth when he got angry.

If you needed medical help in medieval Europe, you might go see the local barber.

TRUE!

Barbers back then were often called barber-surgeons because they might cut you open along with cutting your hair. They often did something called bloodletting—cutting a person to let blood flow out was thought to cure some illnesses. The red and white stripes on today's barber shop poles represent the blood that flowed in the medieval shops, and the white bandages used to stop it. Oh, and medieval barbers also pulled teeth.

Thirteenth-century explorer Marco Polo brought pasta to Italy from China.

FALSE!

Marco (Polo!) did travel to China, and he later wrote about food that was something like pasta. But Italians had already been eating a mixture of flour and water that they molded into different shapes and cooked.

The Roman EMPIRE

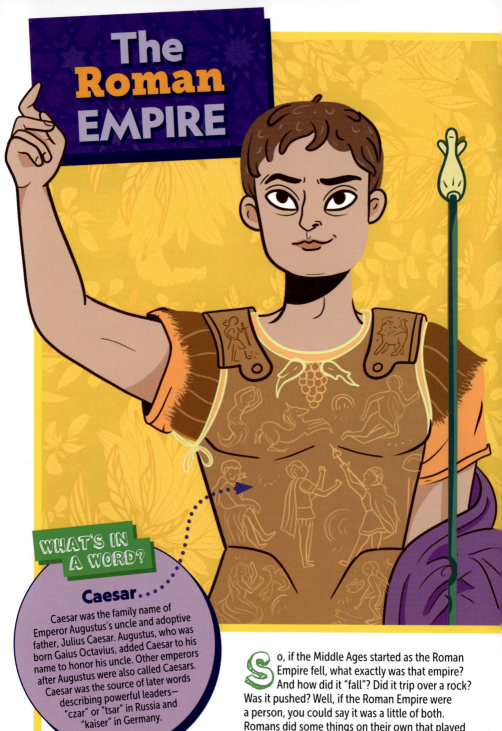

WHAT'S IN A WORD?

Caesar

Caesar was the family name of Emperor Augustus's uncle and adoptive father, Julius Caesar. Augustus, who was born Gaius Octavius, added Caesar to his name to honor his uncle. Other emperors after Augustus were also called Caesars. Caesar was the source of later words describing powerful leaders—"czar" or "tsar" in Russia and "kaiser" in Germany.

So, if the Middle Ages started as the Roman Empire fell, what exactly was that empire? And how did it "fall"? Did it trip over a rock? Was it pushed? Well, if the Roman Empire were a person, you could say it was a little of both. Romans did some things on their own that played a part in ending their empire. It also got a "push" from people who lived outside its borders. But before Rome could fall, it had to rise first.

FROM A CITY TO AN EMPIRE

More than 2,500 years ago, people in a region of Italy called Latium settled in villages near seven hills. These villages became the heart of the city of Rome. At first the Romans were ruled by kings, but in 509 B.C.E., Rome became a republic. Men with wealth worked together to run the government, and common people chose some leaders.

Over the next few centuries, Roman armies defeated neighboring lands. By 200 B.C.E., Rome was on a roll. It controlled all of what is now Italy, Greece, and parts of southern Spain. But the Romans weren't done fighting and expanding. Over the next two centuries. Rome's armies spread out and conquered most of France and parts of North Africa. The growing empire came under the rule of a single powerful person, called an emperor. The first emperor was Augustus Caesar, who came to power in 27 B.C.E.

KEEPING BUSY

What did emperors do? They fought their enemies, built massive buildings, collected taxes, and tried to keep average people fed. By 117 C.E., the Roman Empire reached its greatest size, stretching from England in the north, through southeastern Europe, and into the Middle East. The language spoken in Rome, called Latin, was used throughout the empire. Where they ruled, the Romans built theaters, temples, and other buildings like the ones in their capital city. The empire grew so big that in 285 the emperor Diocletian decided to split it in two. It would be reunited for a time under Constantine the Great.

FAMOUS FOLKS: CONSTANTINE THE GREAT

What made the emperor Constantine (c. 280–337) so great? Well, Rome was facing tough times when Constantine was born—Romans sometimes fought other Romans, and foreign invaders threatened the empire's lands. Constantine had to battle three other Roman leaders to become the sole emperor, in 324. Before then, starting in 313, he had passed laws that helped Christians freely practice their religion. Earlier emperors had tried to restrict Christianity, because the Christians rejected the old Roman gods. Later, Constantine himself became a Christian before he died. His support of the religion helped make it a powerful force in Rome and across Europe after the empire collapsed. On the site of the existing city of Byzantium, he built a new capital, Constantinople (today's Istanbul, Turkey [Türkiye]). After Rome fell, that city became the capital of the Byzantine Empire, which preserved many Roman traditions.

BEFORE THE MIDDLE AGES 27 B.C.E. – 4TH CENTURY C.E. THE ROMAN EMPIRE

11

End of an EMPIRE

After Constantine, there was no guarantee that Rome would forever remain one of the world's most powerful empires. The sheer size of the empire led to problems. When the emperors stopped conquering foreign lands, they took in less money to spend on public projects. And a lot of the money they collected from their citizens (in the form of taxes) went to the military the Caesars had built to protect the empire from foreign attack. They also had to protect themselves from other powerful Romans who wanted their job!

On the empire's farms, wealthy landowners could afford to buy enslaved people to raise their crops and animals. Farmers with less money couldn't afford enslaved people and couldn't produce as much food as the large landowners did. Some had to sell their lands, and they struggled to find work. People who did have jobs had to pay higher and higher taxes.

SPACE INVADERS

But one of the biggest problems Rome faced came from beyond the empire's borders: invaders. The Romans called these invaders "barbarians," because they couldn't understand their languages and because they did not follow Roman customs. Some crossed into Rome seeking protection from warlike tribes that threatened them. Others sought land they could farm or to trade with Roman merchants. And as the western half of the empire weakened, some wanted to rule Roman lands themselves. So, through the 300s and 400s B.C.E., foreign armies flooded into Roman lands from east and west. Many received land from the emperors if they agreed to fight Rome's enemies. Some tribes from what is now Germany were able to set up and rule their own mini-kingdoms within Rome's boundaries. And during the early 400s, some of the Germanic tribes captured large parts of the empire.

The final blow to Roman rule in the western part of the empire came in 476 C.E. A Germanic general named Odoacer rebelled against the last emperor, and his soldiers proclaimed him king of Italy. The Roman Senate agreed to accept Odoacer as their new leader.

WHAT'S IN A WORD?

Barbarian

The Romans borrowed many of their words from the ancient Greeks. *Barbaros* was the Greek word for "foreign," and the Romans had a similar word for peoples who were not part of their empire. Today, someone may be called a barbarian if they act in a violent or rude manner.

These days, if you're a vandal, you're someone who destroys other people's property for no good reason. In Roman times, you might have been a Vandal—a member of the tribe of the same name. Many of the names of the tribes that invaded Rome are still familiar today. Here's a look at some of them.

Know Your Invaders!

THE VANDALS

When the Vandals began knocking on Rome's door—so to speak—they weren't bringing gifts! Starting during the 370s, they were pushed out of their own lands in central Europe, and they eventually took over new land in what is now France. From there, they moved into Spain and North Africa. Their ships terrorized Roman vessels, and in 455, the Vandals attacked the city of Rome itself. The Vandals' kingdom was still around when Rome fell, but the Byzantine Empire later took back the former Roman lands of North Africa.

THE HUNS

One of the peoples of Central Asia who forced the Vandals, and others, to head west were the Huns. Their first homeland was in what is now Mongolia. Fierce fighters on horseback, their most famous leader in Roman times was Attila, who's known today as Attila the Hun. Under his command, the Huns attacked parts of eastern Europe and France. Attila's name is still used today to describe someone who is especially brutal in combat.

THE GOTHS

The Goths took over large parts of the western Roman Empire. They lived in parts of northern Europe and began settling on the Roman frontier during the 200s B.C.E. By the next century, they had split into eastern and western Goths. In 410, the western, or Visigoths, attacked Rome. They later controlled land in what had been Roman France and Spain. During the Middle Ages, the Goths' name was used to describe a type of architecture, called Gothic (see pages 87–89).

BEFORE THE MIDDLE AGES   5TH CENTURY   THE BARBARIAN INVASIONS

Go East, Young ROMAN

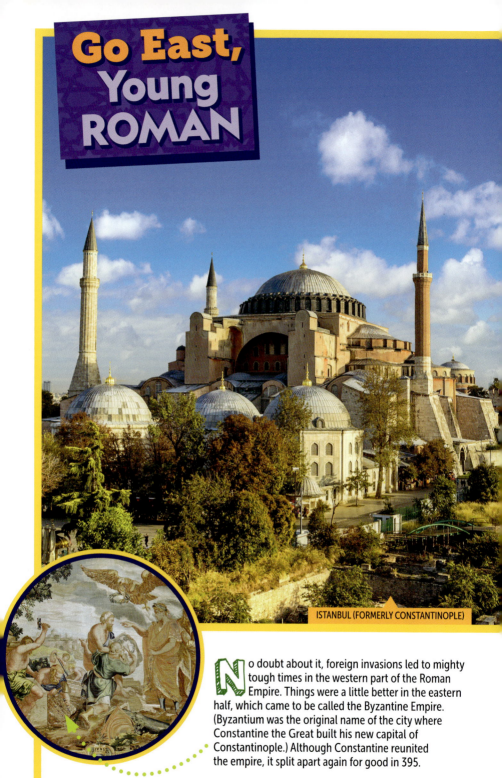

ISTANBUL (FORMERLY CONSTANTINOPLE)

No doubt about it, foreign invasions led to mighty tough times in the western part of the Roman Empire. Things were a little better in the eastern half, which came to be called the Byzantine Empire. (Byzantium was the original name of the city where Constantine the Great built his new capital of Constantinople.) Although Constantine reunited the empire, it split apart again for good in 395.

AN ENDURING EMPIRE

As in the west, the eastern emperors also had to battle some of the Germanic tribes. But the eastern empire was able to hold off many invading foreigners in part by working with them. The eastern leaders gave the Goths and other tribes land and money. This helped the Byzantine Empire survive until the end of the Middle Ages. Over these centuries, its rulers and scholars helped keep alive many of the traditions of the old Roman Empire.

ROMAN, BUT NOT ROMAN

When Constantine built his new capital, he called it New Rome. In some ways, it was better than the old one. Constantinople sat on the Bosporus, a body of water that separates the continents of Asia and Europe. The city had a large harbor and was easy to defend. The new capital was also closer to Egypt, which supplied a lot of the empire's grain. In his new city, Constantine promoted the Christian faith he adopted. He knew, though, that many of the powerful citizens of Rome opposed the religion and still worshipped the old Roman gods.

For a time, the people of the eastern half of the empire considered themselves Roman. Constantinople had buildings and statues like those in Rome, and its libraries were filled with important Roman writings. The people, though, spoke Greek, and the Byzantine Empire became the home of a form of Christianity called Orthodox. It differed in some teachings from the Christian church still based in Rome, which was later called the Roman Catholic Church. The eastern empire also came to be influenced by peoples to its east, such as the Persians.

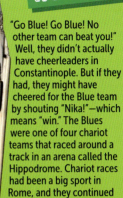

GENTLEMEN, START YOUR HORSES!

"Go Blue! Go Blue! No other team can beat you!" Well, they didn't actually have cheerleaders in Constantinople. But if they had, they might have cheered for the Blue team by shouting "Nika!"—which means "win." The Blues were one of four chariot teams that raced around a track in an arena called the Hippodrome. Chariot races had been a big sport in Rome, and they continued in the Byzantine Empire. The Blues and the Greens dominated the sport, and chariot drivers from the same team would work together to try to make their opponents crash. Everybody seemed to enjoy the races—both common people and the emperor came out to cheer on their favorite team.

BEFORE THE MIDDLE AGES   5TH CENTURY   THE BYZANTINE EMPIRE

ORTHODOX CHURCH

SPOTLIGHT: MONASTIC LIFE

Before the fall of the western Roman Empire, men devoted to Christian beliefs sometimes lived together but apart from the rest of society. They were called monks, and their homes were called monasteries. Monks became important religious figures during the Middle Ages. Here's a look at what they did and how they lived.

DESERT DWELLERS

The earliest monks lived in the deserts of Syria and Egypt. Monks then began building monasteries there and across Europe. One Syrian monastery built in the sixth century had walls up to 115 feet (35 m) high to protect the monks from invaders.

A MONK'S LIFE

Inside the monasteries, monks spent most of their day praying to God or working. Their jobs included raising food and copying ancient writings (see pages 18–19). Some of the writings related to Christian teachings, but others were from Greek and Roman writers who lived before Christianity began. Monks also recorded day-to-day events—they were like the journalists of the Middle Ages.

TEACHING AND PREACHING

Thanks to all the monks' hard work with words, monasteries served as the libraries of the day. They were also schools. Through the first five centuries of the Middle Ages, boys who wanted a good education headed to a monastery. Monks also took care of the sick and aided the poor. And they sometimes ventured outside the monastery walls and became missionaries who tried to persuade more people to become Christians.

A GOOD, GODLY CAREER

Boys as young as five might go to a monastery to begin their education. If they became monks as adults, they knew they would always have a place to live and food to eat. Not everyone could be sure of that during the Middle Ages! Many of the students and monks came from fairly wealthy families. Being a monk was considered a respected career.

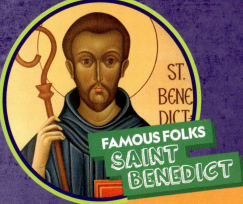

FAMOUS FOLKS
SAINT BENEDICT

Being a monk wasn't easy. For one thing, there were lots of rules to follow. Many of these were first written down by an Italian monk named Saint Benedict of Nursia (480–547). Benedict started several monasteries, and they came to form what is now the Benedictine Order. Benedict said monks had to give up all they owned before they entered the order. They also had to follow all the rules set down by a monastery's main monk, called an abbot, who was chosen by the other monks. Monks were also supposed to talk as little as possible and spend as many as eight hours a day praying. It might seem like it was a tough life, but Benedictine monasteries spread across Europe, and many other orders copied Benedict's rules.

A HAIRCUT ABOVE

It was pretty easy to spot monks. They usually wore a long outer robe with big sleeves. Another robe underneath, called a cowl, had a hood. Monks had shaved heads except for one ring of hair. This distinctive haircut was called a tonsure.

How to Create an
ILLUSTRATED MANUSCRIPT

Monasteries had libraries, but they weren't filled with books like the ones we have today. Instead, the monks produced what are called illuminated manuscripts—and they did them all by hand! If you were a monk, this is how you created an illuminated manuscript.

THE WRITING ROOM

First, you would head to your monastery's scriptorium (a Latin word that means "place for writing"). There, you worked side by side with other monks also copying texts. You were called scribes. The room was not always the most comfortable—it could be hot in the summer and cold in the winter. But you were expected to show up every day, no matter the weather or how you felt.

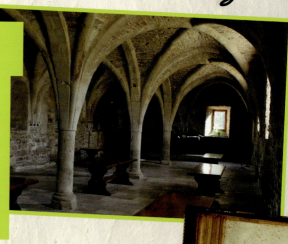

SKIN IS IN

What would you write on? Here's the skinny—you most likely used animal skin as your "paper"! Called parchment, the skin was scraped and stretched and soaked. Then it was covered with a chemical called lime (not the fruit!). Monks preferred calf skin, which was called vellum. Black lines drawn on the vellum helped make sure your sentences were written in straight lines.

THE WRITE STUFF

First you dipped the tip of your pen, which was made from a feather, into black ink. Boiled nuts and tree bark made up the ingredients of some of this ink. After you finished writing, you passed on the vellum to another monk, who added color ink in places. The first letter of a new section of text was usually in color, and the letter was much larger than the ones that followed. The colored inks were made from different chemicals. Illuminated manuscripts also included thin layers of gold called gold leaf.

PARTS OF A PAGE

A single vellum page featured a picture made by an illuminator (which is why we call them illuminated manuscripts). It also had words, of course, and a border filled with decorative designs. The border images might include flowers or animals. Some monks hid little messages in the borders. In one margin note, a monk complained that his parchment still had hair on it!

THE FINISHED PRODUCT

You might have helped create an illuminated manuscript that still exists today. One of the most famous is the Book of Kells. Scottish monks began making it around 800. It features the Gospels, the first four books of the New Testament. Another famous work, a Book of Hours, was created for a French duke in the early 15th century. Books of Hours were prayer books used in private homes.

19

The Power Couple of the EAST

WITNESS TO HISTORY

A Look at the Emperor

"Now in physique [Justinian] was neither tall nor short, but of average height; not thin, but moderately plump; his face was round, and not bad looking, for he had good color, even when he fasted for two days."

—Procopius, *Secret History*

THEODORA AND JUSTINIAN

During the sixth century, monks of the Byzantine Empire could count on support from a pretty important person: Emperor Justinian. He ordered the building of a monastery in Syria that's still used today. Like Constantine, Justinian was sometimes called "the Great." He won important military victories and carried out massive building projects.

The emperor had help ruling his empire. At a time when many royal wives stayed in the background, Empress Theodora played a key role in the government. She welcomed foreign leaders and helped Justinian shape some of his policies.

THE PATH TO GREATNESS

People might not have expected much from young Petrus Sabbatius, better known today as Justinian. Petrus was born around 483 in what is now Serbia. He headed to Constantinople for his education. His uncle Justin served there as head of the emperor's guards. In 518, Justin became emperor, and in 527, he asked his nephew to rule with him. Petrus then took the name Justinian, and he became the sole emperor later that year after his uncle's death.

FROM THE STAGE TO THE THRONE

Like her husband, Theodora did not come from royal blood. Born around 500, she was an actress who caught Justinian's eye. He soon saw one of the benefits of being the emperor's nephew: In 523, he managed to have a law changed that had kept upper-class citizens from marrying common people like Theodora. And he must have been glad he did. As he ruled, Justinian basically told the people, "Whatever I say, goes." That upset many citizens of Constantinople, and in 532, they began to riot. Justinian thought about fleeing the mob, which wanted a new emperor. Theodora, though, said not so fast. She urged him to fight to keep his title. He did, and he ruled for another 33 years.

PETRUS SABBATIUS SPOKE LATIN, BUT HE NEVER REALLY MASTERED GREEK, WHICH WAS MORE COMMONLY USED IN THE BYZANTINE EMPIRE.

LAYING DOWN THE LAW

One of Justinian's greatest feats was creating a series of legal documents known today as the Justinian Code. He had some of the empire's great "legal eagles" go through old Roman laws and weed out any that contradicted other laws. The code also included new laws passed during Justinian's rule. Theodora had a hand in introducing laws that helped women. One of the new laws gave divorced women more legal rights. Another said women, for the first time, could own and inherit property.

THEODORA'S FATHER TRAINED A BEAR THAT ENTERTAINED AUDIENCES IN THE HIPPODROME.

Call my agent.

THE BYZANTINE EMPIRE · 6TH CENTURY · JUSTINIAN & THEODORA

SUCCESS ON THE BATTLEFIELD

Justinian was no warrior, but he knew enough to hire good generals. With their help, Justinian was able to win control of Roman lands that had fallen to foreign invaders. Starting in 534, the emperor's armies took back parts of North Africa, Spain, and Italy. Justinian also ordered the rebuilding of a church in Constantinople called the Hagia Sophia (Greek for "holy wisdom"; see page 86). Theodora used some of the empire's wealth to support other churches.

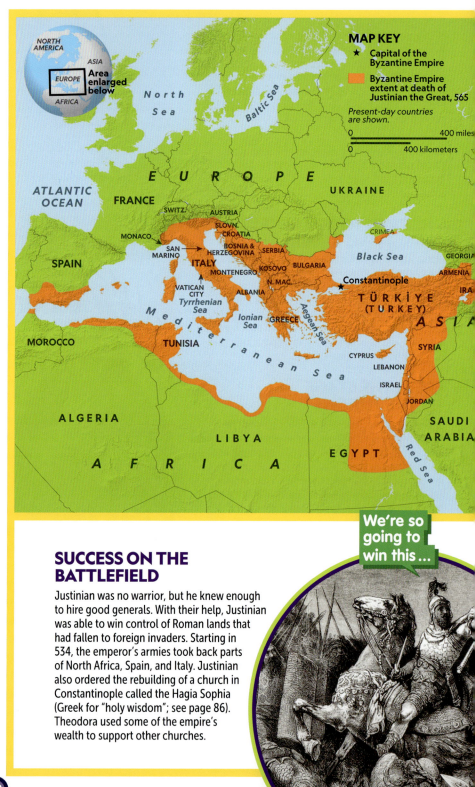

We're so going to win this ...

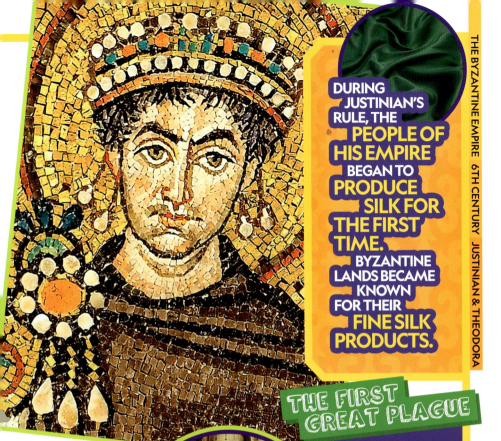

THE BYZANTINE EMPIRE   6TH CENTURY   JUSTINIAN & THEODORA

DURING JUSTINIAN'S RULE, THE **PEOPLE OF HIS EMPIRE** BEGAN TO **PRODUCE SILK FOR THE FIRST TIME.** BYZANTINE LANDS BECAME KNOWN FOR THEIR **FINE SILK PRODUCTS.**

THE FIRST GREAT PLAGUE

You may have heard of a disease called the bubonic plague, which killed millions of people through medieval Europe and Asia during the 14th century (see pages 124–127). About 800 years earlier, Justinian saw the plague sweep across his lands, with deadly effect. The disease broke out in North Africa in 541 and reached Constantinople the next year. The death toll rose to between 5,000 and 10,000 every day—even cats and dogs lost their lives to the plague! Some people thought the disease was the work of God; others said they saw spirits right before they became sick. Scientists now know that a bacterium, not God or spirits, causes the disease. The plague's impact on Constantinople weakened after just a few months, but people in other parts of the empire, and beyond, battled the disease for several centuries.

TROUBLE AT THE END

Theodora died in 548. Justinian ruled for another 17 years, but by the time of his death, in 565, the Byzantine Empire had lost some of its shine. Justinian's military adventures in the west weakened the empire's other borders, opening the door to future foreign invasions. And the high taxes Justinian collected upset many of the empire's citizens. Still, under Justinian and Theodora, the Byzantine Empire reached the peak of its power.

23

A COMPETING EMPIRE

As if disease and warfare weren't bad enough, Justinian and Theodora had to worry about a powerful empire to the east. The Sassanian Empire was centered in Persia, an ancient term for a region in Asia that included modern Iran. Starting in the third century B.C.E., the Sassanians battled the Roman Empire for land, and this warfare continued against the Byzantine Empire. The two sides fought during the early years of Justinian's rule. In the early 600s, the Sassanians were able to take back land they had previously lost to the Byzantine Empire.

A THIRD EMPIRE

The Sassanians followed two older Persian empires. The first rose before Rome, in the sixth century B.C.E., and the second came to power during the second century B.C.E. Sassanian leaders wanted to restore the glory of these former empires.

During the sixth century, one leader, Khosrow I, led the Sassanians successfully and consolidated the power of the empire. He was nicknamed Khosrow the Just. Just what? Just about the best king the Sassanians ever had! Finishing what his father Kawad I started, he made tax collection just—meaning more fair—and gave land back to farmers that earlier Sassanian rulers had taken away. Khosrow also improved his empire's army, which relied on a skilled cavalry.

HERE'S THE POINT

Joust about everyone knows medieval knights competed in jousting tournaments. But they might not know that, centuries earlier, Sassanian warriors fought on horseback using weapons called lances. The first jousts were part of combat. Armed with a lance, a Sassanian soldier would challenge an enemy soldier to fight, one on one. These early jousts appear in rock carvings about 1,800 years old. Later, some of the wealthy men of the empire also enjoyed jousting for sport. During the 11th century, European knights began to hold jousting tournaments (see pages 100–101).

DAILY LIFE

The Sassanian rulers and their people practiced an ancient Persian religion called Zoroastrianism. This religion taught that there was one powerful god, and people could go to either heaven or hell after they died, depending on how well they acted in life. Sassanian merchants and traders purchased goods in China and brought them to the Sassanian Empire. The goods included spices and weapons. When Khosrow ruled, he promoted the arts and education. His silversmiths were well known for their skills. And Khosrow welcomed Greek and Indian scholars into the empire.

THE SASSANIANS' FOES OFTEN SAW LARGE, LUMBERING BEASTS COMING AT THEM— ELEPHANTS! FOR CENTURIES, PERSIAN ARMIES USED THEM IN BATTLE.

MEDIEVAL ASIA 3RD CENTURY - 7TH CENTURY THE SASSANIAN EMPIRE

25

SPOTLIGHT: THE SILK ROAD

WHO TRADED WHAT?

A road made of silk? How could it stand up to the rolling of wagon wheels and the stomping feet of pack animals? Easy—the road wasn't really made of silk. It had rocks and dirt, and at times it had water, too. But silk was one of the first and most important goods carried by traders who traveled the road, which linked China to Europe.

The variety of goods carried along the Silk Road could fill a modern superstore. Traders in Central Asia sent horses packed with goods east to China. Along with silk, Chinese merchants sent all sorts of spices west, including cinnamon, cloves, nutmeg, and ginger. They also sent items made from porcelain, a kind of ceramic. India sent cloth, ivory, and pearls. Sassanian traders carried items made of bronze and silver. And in Europe, traders sent wool, olive oil, and other items east. The people of what are now Russia and Scandinavia sent honey, furs, and wood. Constantinople was a key spot on the Silk Road. Several different trade routes came together there.

Area enlarged below

MAP KEY
— Major Silk Road route
• Historic city of interest

Present-day countries are shown.

0   600 miles
0   600 kilometers

A ROUTE WITH DEEP ROOTS

The Silk Road passed through both the Byzantine and Sassanian Empires. But the trade between the East and West along this road had begun long before. Chinese merchants had used some of these routes for centuries, but the pace of trade picked up during the second century B.C.E. Merchants left from the city of Chang'an, which was then the Chinese capital. Silk was the most valuable item they carried, since at the time no one outside China knew how to make this beautiful cloth.

The road was actually a series of paths and trails, and it sometimes included sea routes on the Indian Ocean and the Persian Gulf. Traders joined together to form caravans, because there was safety in numbers. The authorities in China and other countries along the road couldn't always protect the merchants. Travelers also had to cross deserts and trudge over snowy mountains. A merchant didn't travel the whole route—they sold some of their goods along the way, and other merchants continued to carry them west. They also brought goods back to China.

ALONG THE SILK ROAD

"Both hills and valleys are filled with snow piles, and it freezes both in spring and summer; if it should thaw for a time, the ice soon forms again. The roads are steep and dangerous, the cold wind is extremely biting …"

—Xuanzang, *Record of the Western Regions*

MORE THAN SILK AND SPICES

People traveling the Silk Road brought more than food and luxury goods with them. At times, they also spread deadly diseases such as smallpox and bubonic plague. The travelers also brought inventions from one area to another, including a new and improved plow for farming that spread from Asia to Europe. And missionaries from different religions traveled the road to spread their faiths. Indian merchants along the road introduced Buddhism to new lands, particularly China. Christians and Muslims also traveled parts of the route and shared their beliefs.

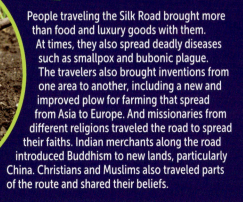

The Prophet for a New RELIGION

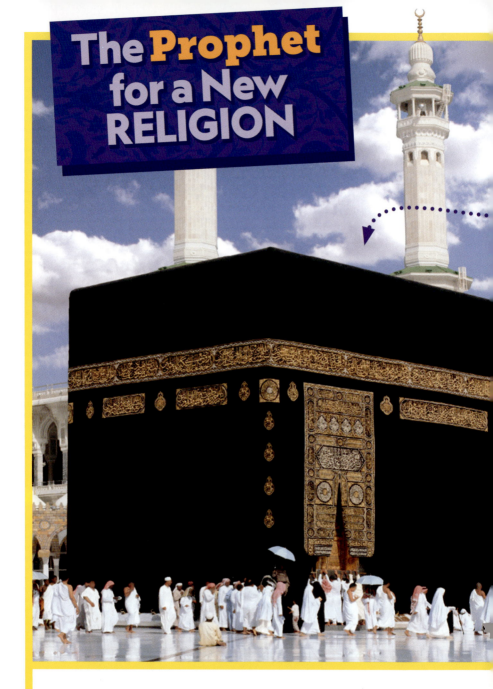

Would anyone have guessed that a young shepherd, born around 570 and then orphaned, would grow up to spark the start of a new religion? And that the religion would eventually spread around the globe, with more than 1.5 billion followers? Maybe not, but it actually happened to Muhammad. He is known as one of God's messengers, or the Prophet of Islam.

VISITS FROM AN ANGEL

Muhammad was born in the city of Mecca, in what is now Saudi Arabia. At the time, some people of the region were nomads. Others lived in villages and worked as traders. The major empires to the north largely ignored them. The nomads and others gathered in Mecca to worship a number of gods.

When Muhammad was about 40, he saw a vision of the angel Gabriel. The people of the region were familiar with the teachings of Christianity and Judaism. Gabriel is an angel from the Bible. He told Muhammad to worship God, or Allah, as the one true god. Muhammad began to share the messages he received from Gabriel, which led to a new religion called Islam. This Arabic word means "surrender." Members of the faith, called Muslims, were supposed to surrender to the will of their god, Allah. Some of Muhammad's followers wrote down the messages he received from Gabriel. This became the Islamic holy book, the Quran. Muhammad's teachings were also written down.

FLEEING AND RETURNING

Muhammad upset some people from his own tribes by saying they should worship only Allah. And the wealthy disliked his calls to help the poor. After being treated poorly in Mecca, in 622, Muhammad and the people who accepted Islam left for a city called Medina. Several years later, Muhammad and his followers began to carry out raids against caravans. After one attack against a caravan from Mecca, the residents of that city fought back. The two sides battled, and Muhammad won several victories. Over the next few years, more people accepted Islam and considered Muhammad their political and religious leader. In 630, he marched on Mecca with an army of 10,000 men and took over the city.

FAMILIAR FIGURES

Some of the religious figures who appear in the Quran also appear in earlier religious writings. Some are mentioned in the Old Testament, or the Hebrew Bible, one of the holy texts of Judaism. Others are mentioned in the New Testament, which describes the life of Jesus Christ and the rise of Christianity. Muslims believe that Islam, Judaism, and Christianity share a common ancient prophet: Abraham. He appears in the Quran and the Old Testament. Other figures from the Old Testament mentioned in the Quran include Adam and Moses. The Quran also lists Jesus as one of the great prophets before Muhammad and devotes a chapter to his mother, Mary (called Maryam in Arabic). But Muslims don't believe he was the son of God, as Christians do.

ISLAMIC LANDS 570-632 PROPHET MUHAMMAD

The Rise of ISLAM

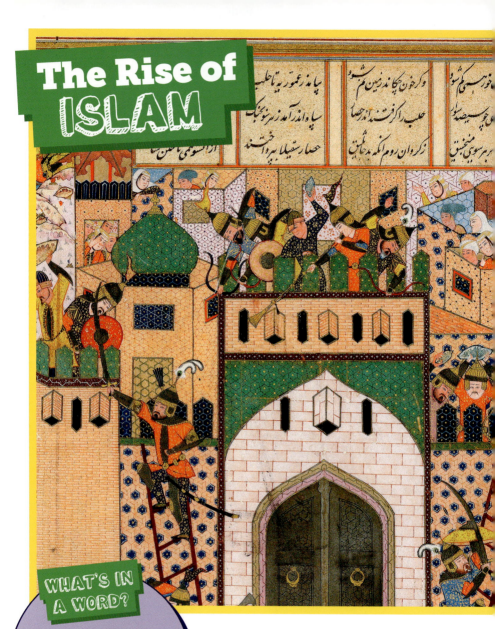

WHAT'S IN A WORD?

Caliph
"Caliph" comes from the Arabic word *khalifah*, which means "successor," or the person who takes over after an existing leader dies or is replaced. A caliphate is the lands a caliph rules.

Was Muhammad done trying to spread the new Islamic faith? No—he had only just begun! For a time, he attracted new followers in part because of the strength of his army. Local leaders promised their loyalty to Muhammad without him firing a shot. Then, later in 630, he set out with an even bigger army and marched north toward Syria. Once again, he found many people who agreed to accept Islam and follow his rule.

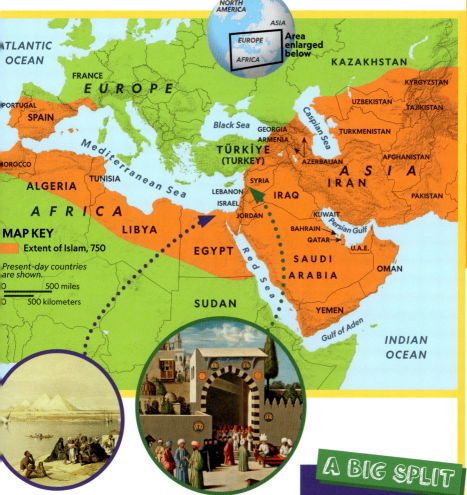

ISLAMIC LANDS 570 - 632 PROPHET MUHAMMAD

ON THE GO

Muhammad died in 632. But his followers continued to spread Islam, and they were ready to fight to do it. That meant clashing with the Byzantine and Sassanian Empires, which controlled lands surrounding the territory Muhammad had won. In 635, Muslim armies took the Byzantine city of Damascus, in Syria. Over the next decade, the armies went as far west as Egypt, winning battles along the way. They also pushed into Persian lands and continued heading east. In 664, they seized Kabul, the capital of what is now Afghanistan.

The leaders who followed Muhammad kept winning battles and conquering new lands into the eighth century. By 750, the Sassanian Empire was long gone, and the Byzantine Empire had shrunk. Muslim leaders controlled a new empire that stretched from Spain to Central Asia.

A BIG SPLIT

Muhammad died with no sons to take over the lands he controlled. Some Muslim leaders then chose the Prophet's father-in-law, Abu Bakr, to become caliph. He would rule over the Muslim lands and be a religious leader as well. But other Muslims wanted Muhammad's cousin and son-in-law, Ali, to become caliph. He did, but the Muslims remained divided. The opposing sides eventually fought a civil war that lasted for decades. In the end, the followers of Islam divided into two branches, and that division remains today. The Muslims who say Abu Bakr was the true caliph are called Sunnis. The ones who back Ali's claim are called Shiites.

31

A NEW WESTERN POWER

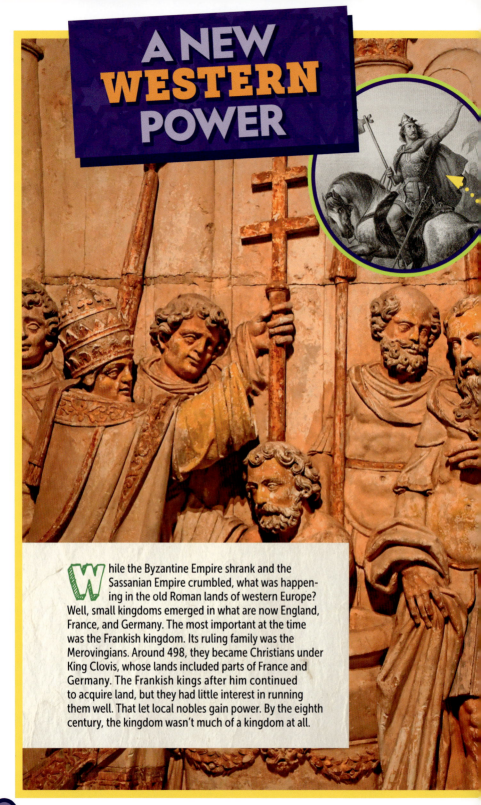

While the Byzantine Empire shrank and the Sassanian Empire crumbled, what was happening in the old Roman lands of western Europe? Well, small kingdoms emerged in what are now England, France, and Germany. The most important at the time was the Frankish kingdom. Its ruling family was the Merovingians. Around 498, they became Christians under King Clovis, whose lands included parts of France and Germany. The Frankish kings after him continued to acquire land, but they had little interest in running them well. That let local nobles gain power. By the eighth century, the kingdom wasn't much of a kingdom at all.

IT'S HAMMER TIME

One of these local leaders was Charles Martel. His last name came from an Old French word meaning "hammer." His father, Pépin, had the title of mayor of the palace for the eastern part of the Frankish kingdom. Charles took over this position in 718. While Merovingian kings still sat on the throne, Charles Martel was the real power in the eastern kingdom. He raised armies to fight his rival, the mayor of the palace of the western half of Frankish lands. After defeating his enemy, Charles was in charge of the whole kingdom, though he never took the title of king. He also had to give some of the local princes freedom to rule their own lands as they chose.

A superb soldier, Charles sent troops to battle tribes in Germany. He also knew it helped to have friends, so he won the support of important officials in the Roman Catholic Church. After Charles died, his son Pépin the Short won the approval of the pope in Rome to be officially crowned king. That took place in 751. It marked the start of the Carolingian dynasty. The name came from the Latin version of "Charles." Pépin's biggest claim to fame was being the father of history's next great emperor: Charlemagne.

Can't touch this.

A BIG BATTLE

While Charles Martel was in power, the Franks faced a huge threat from Muslims based in Spain. Muslim armies had conquered the region several decades before, and now they had crossed the Pyrenees mountains and entered southern France. With the aid of a French duke, Charles led his troops into battle against the Muslims. The two sides met near Tours, France, in October 732. Charles's men stood firm against a Muslim assault before launching their own attack. His army eventually stopped the Muslim advance. Charles's victory impressed other Europeans, who began to think of themselves as united because of their Christian faith.

MEDIEVAL EUROPE   5TH CENTURY - 8TH CENTURY   THE FRANKS

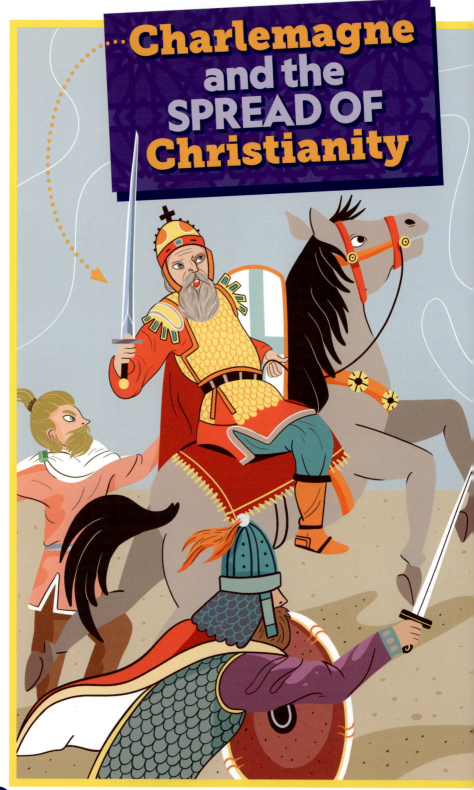

Charles's son Pépin was called "the Short," but nobody could say that about one of his sons. Like his grandfather, this son was named Charles, and he was about six feet (1.8 m) tall. Thanks to his long and successful reign, he earned the nickname Charles the Great. We know him better today as Charlemagne, which comes from the Latin *Carolus Magnus*, meaning—you guessed it—Charles the Great.

Charlemagne took over his father's realm in 771. He soon proved his skill on the battlefield, leading armies against the Lombards of Italy and seizing their kingdom. His armies also raided other lands, taking treasures. And in 778, Charlemagne ventured across the Pyrenees to fight Muslim armies, but he came back without any major victories.

THE PESKY SAXONS

For more than 30 years, Charlemagne and his troops fought against the Saxons of northern Germany. Some Saxons had broken their earlier promise to be loyal to the Frankish kings. Charlemagne made them pay by conquering their lands. He also forced the Saxons to accept Christianity. Like his father and grandfather, Charlemagne had a good relationship with the current pope in Rome, and he sometimes sent his troops to defend lands controlled by the pope.

A NEW EMPEROR

By 800, Pope Leo III saw that Charlemagne was a friend of the church, as well as one wonderful warrior. On Christmas Day that year, Leo crowned him emperor of the Romans, chosen by God to rule much of the old Roman lands. With this move, Leo hoped to create a second Christian empire distinct from the Byzantine Empire. And with that second empire, Leo hoped the church would have greater influence over western Europe. The empire Charlemagne controlled would come to be called the Holy Roman Empire. At the time of his death in 814, it stretched from northern Spain across France to central Europe and included half of Italy.

CHARLEMAGNE HAD GOOD RELATIONS WITH HARUN AL-RASHID, THE MUSLIM CALIPH BASED IN BAGHDAD. HARUN SENT CHARLEMAGNE MANY GIFTS, INCLUDING A GOLD TRAY, A CLOCK POWERED BY WATER, AND AN ELEPHANT.

MEDIEVAL EUROPE C. 742 - 814 CHARLEMAGNE

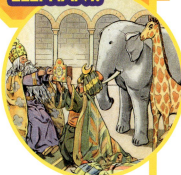

AN ANGLE ON THE SAXONS

The Saxons were another Germanic tribe that had threatened the old Roman Empire. Based along the North and Baltic Seas, they sometimes carried out pirate raids. By the time Charlemagne came to power, they had settled as far west as England. There, they joined with tribes called the Angles and the Jutes to control parts of that land. The Saxons began to speak the language of the Angles, whose name is the root for the word "English." The Saxons are still around today—or at least their name is. The term Anglo-Saxon is sometimes used to describe the period of English history from the early fifth century to 1066.

35

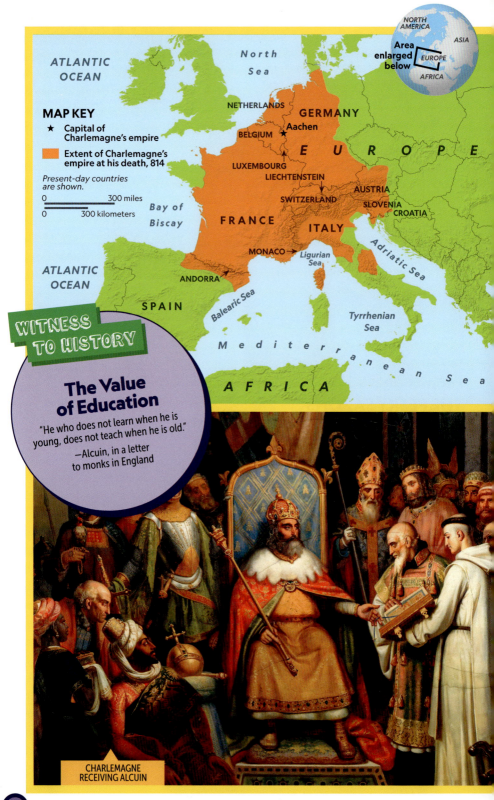

MAP KEY
★ Capital of Charlemagne's empire
▮ Extent of Charlemagne's empire at his death, 814

Present-day countries are shown.

WITNESS TO HISTORY

The Value of Education

"He who does not learn when he is young, does not teach when he is old."

—Alcuin, in a letter to monks in England

CHARLEMAGNE RECEIVING ALCUIN

MORE THAN A WARRIOR

Charlemagne's military successes built his empire. But the emperor was more than just a battler. While he couldn't read and write for most of his life, Charlemagne learned how to speak Greek and Latin, and he asked educated men to read books to him. In his capital of Aachen, he started a school and a library, and he encouraged learning and the arts across the empire. Helping Charlemagne was an English educator named Alcuin. He came to the emperor's court and led the effort to start new schools. His and Charlemagne's work created what's been called the Carolingian Renaissance, which occurred from the late eighth century to the ninth century. Charlemagne wanted to bring back knowledge from Roman times and spread it across his realm.

RUNNING AN EMPIRE

Charlemagne also had to actually *rule* his empire, which meant working with local nobles. He gave them land to win their loyalty. In return, he expected the nobles to fight for him when he called on them. They also had to make sure they kept roads and bridges in good repair. Charlemagne was considered a fair ruler, and his people respected him.

But the empire he built didn't last long. After Charlemagne died in 814, his son Louis the Pious became sole emperor. He kept the realm together until his own death, in 840. But after that, the empire began to split apart. The title of Holy Roman Emperor remained, but it was not much of an empire.

A NEW CAPITAL

If Constantine and Justinian could build great capital cities, Charlemagne thought he could, too. He chose an ancient town called Aachen for his home base. It's located in Germany near the modern-day border with Belgium and the Netherlands. Here, Charlemagne built a palace and a cathedral. He brought in builders from across his realm and took art from other churches to decorate his new one. Aachen was a capital for only about 50 years, until Charlemagne's grandsons divided the empire three ways, and each chose a new capital. But future German kings and queens were crowned in the cathedral Charlemagne built. A part of the cathedral, called the Palatine Chapel, still stands. It's the best preserved building from the Carolingian Renaissance.

SCHOLARS WORKING FOR CHARLEMAGNE PERFECTED A NEW WAY TO WRITE. THEY USED BOTH CAPITAL AND LOWERCASE LETTERS FOR THE FIRST TIME AND PUT IN SPACES BETWEEN WORDS.

SPOTLIGHT: FARMING

Who kept the people of the Middle Ages fed? Farmers, of course. And they raised crops without the computers and monster pieces of equipment many of today's farmers use. But Middle Age farmers did develop new technology and farming methods that made life easier—and led to more food for everyone.

WHICH FOODS WHERE?

What foods cropped up on medieval farms? Here's a look at just a few.

Egypt was a "breadbasket" for several empires, providing wheat. Northern Europeans also raised wheat, as well as barley and rye. Warm regions in southern Europe grew grapes for wine and olives for oil. One crop that crossed several continents was eggplant. From India, traders took it west across Asia to Europe and Africa. Of course, the great medieval empires of Asia, Africa, and Europe didn't have all the foods loved today. Corn, potatoes, tomatoes, and the beans that give us chocolate were found only in the Americas. It wasn't until after 1492 that Europeans began spreading them around the world.

EGYPT: wheat

NORTHERN EUROPE: wheat, barley, and rye

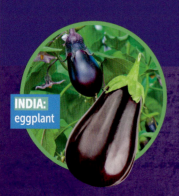
INDIA: eggplant

SOUTHERN EUROPE: grapes for wine and olives for oil

38

FROM TWO FIELDS TO THREE

Letting a field go fallow means not planting crops on it for a season. That way, the soil doesn't lose all its nutrients. For centuries, farmers used a two-field system. They planted half their land with crops and let the other half go fallow. But starting around 1000, European farmers had a bright idea: They split their lands into thirds. One field was fallow, while one was used for a main crop, such as wheat. On the new, third field, they planted legumes, such as peas and clover. These crops actually put nutrients back into the soil, and the farmers could use the crops to feed themselves or their animals. The three-field system let farmers raise more crops than ever before.

NO HORSING AROUND

What was another big breakthrough down on the farm? Horseshoes! These iron shoes help protect horses' feet while they work. Starting around 1000 or so, Europeans also began breeding stronger horses that were better able to pull a plow. They were harder, faster workers than the oxen that farmers had used. Oxen wore collars around their necks that were connected to the plows they pulled. But these collars didn't fit right on horses, so around 1100, farmers designed collars that were a better fit. This made plowing easier than ever, and horses became workhorses on the farm.

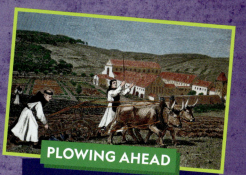

PLOWING AHEAD

And what about the plows the oxen and horses pulled? Were they all alike? *Neigh!* Sometime after 800, a new plow appeared on farms in parts of Europe. This "heavy plow" broke up the soil, like other plows did. But then it turned over the dug-up earth and created a row where farmers could plant their seeds. This meant they could start planting with less work. These new plows were also perfect for digging up the thick, clay soils of northern Europe, making farming easier there. Some farmers then put wheels on their plows, which made them easier for horses to pull.

39

Victorious VIKINGS

WHAT'S IN A WORD?
Yule be happy to know that some of our English words trace their roots to the old Norse language—like "yule" and "happy." Another is "Thursday," which comes from the name of the Norse god Thor.

VIKING TRAINING FOR BATTLE INCLUDED PLAYING **TUG-OF-WAR.** THIS TRAINING WAS **SERIOUS BUSINESS,** SINCE THE **LOSING TEAM** GOT PULLED INTO A **PIT OF FIRE!**

DEPICTION OF VIKING SETTLERS EXPLORING THE NORTH AMERICAN COAST

WITNESS TO HISTORY

Deadly Raids

"[The Vikings] came with a naval force to Britain like stinging hornets and spread on all sides like fearful wolves ... and they came to the church of Lindisfarne ... and seized all the treasures of the holy church."

—Simeon of Durham, *Historia Regum*

GOING BERSERK IN BATTLE

While Charlemagne was building his empire, parts of Europe faced a new threat from the north. During the eighth century, warriors from Norway, Sweden, and Denmark began to sail out on long wooden ships. When they came ashore on foreign lands, they struck quickly and violently, raiding monasteries and towns before returning home. These "Norsemen," now better known as Vikings, were not to the liking of the people they attacked!

MORE THAN WARRIORS

The Vikings' raids are what many people remember about them today. Most took place in the British Isles, France, Germany, and Russia. But the Vikings were much more than just brutal robbers. They settled in some of the lands they attacked, and for a time they ruled England. They were also traders. They used rivers to set up trade routes that stretched from the Baltic Sea near Scandinavia to the Caspian Sea, bordering the Byzantine Empire. Viking craftspeople made beautiful items, and the Vikings created their own form of writing, using characters called runes.

At home and where they settled, most Norse were farmers. Society was split into slaves at the bottom, a large number of free common folks, and a small number of wealthy and powerful leaders at the top. Women were in charge of the home, and some ran farms. In Viking towns and trading centers, women sometimes played a role in business, too. Unlike women in other parts of Europe, Viking women could own land, and if they wanted a divorce, all they had to do was tell people, "I want a divorce."

Sure, Vikings could thrust a spear or swing a battle-ax as well as anyone. But Vikings called berserkers really went wild on the battlefield. Sometimes they were called wolfskins, but by any name, they were fierce fighters. They wore animal skins and howled like wolves as they engaged their enemies. Legends said that fire didn't hurt them, and they couldn't feel pain. They got so pumped up before a battle that some would bite their shields—or even take a swing at their own soldiers! The first written records of berserkers date to the ninth century. One berserker guarding a narrow wooden bridge during a battle in 1066 is said to have slowed the advance of the English by cutting down more than 40 soldiers with his battle-ax (before a soldier went under the bridge and killed him with a spear).

MEDIEVAL EUROPE 8TH CENTURY – 11TH CENTURY THE VIKING AGE

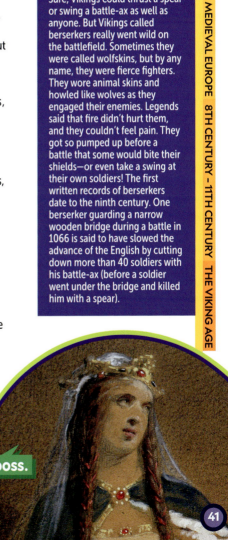

I'm a boss.

41

THE VIKING WORLD

Map

MAP KEY
→ Viking trade, settlement, and attack route
■ Area settled by Vikings
■ Area under Viking influence

Present-day countries are shown.

0 — 800 miles
0 — 800 kilometers

Labeled locations: CANADA, Labrador Sea, Island of Newfoundland, GREENLAND (DENMARK), Greenland Sea, ICELAND, Norwegian Sea, ARCTIC OCEAN, FINLAND, SWEDEN, NORWAY, Ladoga, Novgorod, EST., LATV., LITH., RUSS., BELARUS, POLAND, DENMARK, GERMANY, NETH., North Sea, UNITED KINGDOM, Dublin, IRELAND (ÉIRE), ATLANTIC OCEAN, Rouen, Normandy, FRANCE, SPAIN, Seville, MOROCCO, Mediterranean

Where to next?

Dublin, Ireland

The luck of the Irish ran out when the Vikings came 'round. In 837, the Norsemen launched a major invasion of Ireland, with more than 100 of their famous longships coming ashore. A few years later, they began to settle there. They first built Dublin as a fort, but it later became a trading center. The Vikings built ships in Dublin, and items found in their graves there include swords and tools.

Ladoga, Russia

Around 855, Vikings settled in this town. The Vikings there were called Rus, and several centuries later, the area was called Russia after them. Under their leader Rurik, the Rus founded Novgorod, which became early Russia's first capital. Viking trade routes in this area connected Scandinavia and the Middle East.

LEIF ERIKSSON

42

Normandy, France

In 911, a Viking named Rollo and his men received land from the French king Charles the Simple. They settled in part of northern France near the city of Rouen. From their new home, the Vikings carried out raids in Italy. The Viking settlement in France became known as the land of the Northmen, the source of the region's name that is still used today—Normandy. The people of Normandy were called Normans, and they would play a big role in English history.

Seville, Spain

The Viking raids reached into Muslim lands as well. In 844, Danish Vikings sailed along the coast of Spain and captured the city of Seville. In a battle that followed, Muslim forces and the invaders fought just outside the city. The Muslims defeated the Danes and killed several hundred men they took as prisoners. About 15 years later, Viking ships sailed along the coast of North Africa, which was also under Muslim control.

Iceland

Here are the cold facts—Vikings sailed west and settled in Iceland around 874. Less than 100 years later, about 25,000 Vikings were living there. Their government included one of the world's first parliaments, called the Althing. The Vikings had a tradition of having free men come together in towns and villages to decide how things should be run. But Iceland's Althing was no small thing—it made laws for the whole country.

Greenland

For some of the Icelandic Vikings, the urge (or the pressure) to keep going west led them to sail to Greenland around 982. Erik the Red got into trouble in Iceland and was forced to leave. He and his family then decided to sail west, to lands Erik had heard about. His voyage led to the settlement of Greenland, and other Icelanders followed. To sail across the ocean, the Vikings relied on knowing the sun's position at noon for each week of the year. Some sailors also raved about ravens—one story says that they let loose the birds and followed them. Ravens were thought to be able to wing their way toward land.

Newfoundland

Erik the Red's son Leif Eriksson set off from Greenland and made history. He and his crew reached what is now Newfoundland, in eastern Canada, around 1000. They became the first Europeans to reach North America. And in a sad sign of things to come, the Europeans fought and killed some of the Native people they met there. The settlement Leif founded was discovered in 1960. Some say the Vikings explored even more of North America.

43

BURY Interesting Graves

The Vikings used their longships to carry out raids and trade. But they also hauled some of the ships on land and used them for the burials of important people. Let's dig into some of the medieval burial sites found in modern times—and the riches they held.

FOUND IN A MOUND

Mounds marking where Vikings were buried are scattered all over Scandinavia. In 1879, two teenagers in Sandefjord, Norway, began digging into one of the mounds. What they found were the remains of a Viking burial ship, known today as the Gokstad ship. Made of oak, the ship was about 78 feet (24 m) long and once carried a crew of 34 men. An important warrior wounded in battle sometime around 900 was buried inside the ship. Placed near him were all sorts of items he might need as he traveled to the land of the dead, including a bed, a sleigh, and small boats. And the warrior wasn't buried alone—archaeologists also discovered the remains of animals, including horses, dogs, and peacocks!

LEADING LADIES

In 1903, a farmer in Slagen, Norway, found a small piece of wood in a burial mound. His discovery led to the uncovering of another Viking burial ship. This one was even better preserved than the Gokstad ship, and it was a little longer, too. Thieves had stolen many items from the Oseberg ship before it was discovered, but they left behind the bones of two people. Recent research has shown that the bones belonged to women. Because only important Vikings were buried in ships, it's likely that these women were royalty or important religious figures. The items found with their bones included a small cart and five finely carved wooden animal heads.

USING **RADAR** DIRECTED INTO THE GROUND, **ARCHAEOLOGISTS** IN 2018 FOUND THE REMAINS OF ANOTHER **VIKING BURIAL SHIP** IN NORWAY. IN 2020, THEY BEGAN **DIGGING UP** THE SHIP. THIS WORK **UNCOVERED** MORE VIKING REMAINS, INCLUDING A FARMHOUSE AND A HALL FOR **CELEBRATIONS.**

A GRAVE FIT FOR A KING

Hoo knew that the Anglo-Saxons buried their kings in ships? Well, now you do. And some of the proof comes from a spot in England called Sutton Hoo. Starting in 1938, archaeologists uncovered the burial site of a king dating from the early 600s. Inside the grave was silverware made of real silver, an iron helmet, a gold belt buckle, and much more. The scientists could also tell that these items and the king had been placed inside a wooden ship at the site, but the wood had turned to dust by the time Sutton Hoo was found. This was the second burial ship discovered in England.

HIDDEN TOMB ROOM

Not all medieval burials took place in ships, of course. In 2003, archaeologists found a burial chamber in Prittlewell, England, that dated back to the end of the sixth century. It was the final resting place of a wealthy Anglo-Saxon man; buried with him were gold coins and crosses, bronze cooking pots, and copper buckles. Inside were also the remains of a stringed instrument called a lyre, containing gems that had likely come from as far away as India.

45

My, My, MAYA

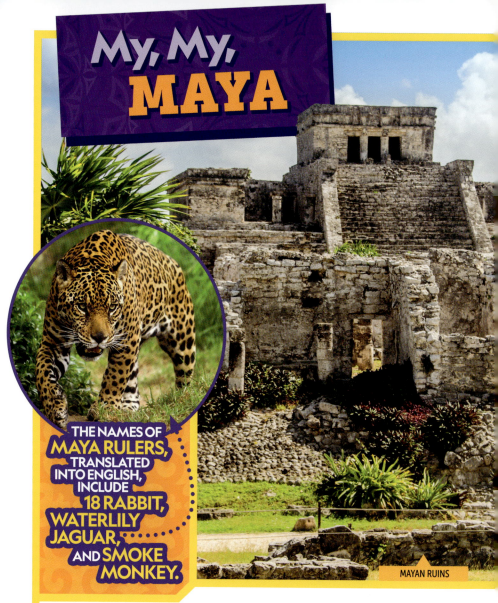

MAYAN RUINS

THE NAMES OF **MAYA RULERS**, TRANSLATED INTO ENGLISH, INCLUDE **18 RABBIT, WATERLILY JAGUAR,** AND **SMOKE MONKEY.**

Behold, my brilliance!

While Vikings sailed the seas, and Muslims and Christians spread their faith, a powerful people controlled parts of Mexico and Central America. They were the Maya, and they were the only people in that part of the world at that time who developed a system of writing. They also built great cities, studied the movement of the planets and the stars, and created calendars.

A NATION OF CITIES

The Maya began to farm and build cities long before the start of the Middle Ages. One of their major cities, Copán, was first settled around 1000 B.C.E. But the Maya reached their peak during the seventh and eighth centuries C.E. They were not a single country with a single ruler. Instead, the Maya built different independent cities, each with its own king. The largest cities had populations of more than 50,000! The kings from the different cities sometimes battled each other for power. Capturing enemy soldiers was a major goal of Maya warfare. The prisoners were often killed as sacrifices to the Maya gods.

LIFE IN MAYA TIMES

The Maya raised several important crops, such as corn, beans, and chilies, and dug canals to bring water to their fields. They thought the position of certain planets and stars could help them predict the future, so educated Maya advised the kings based on what they saw in the night sky. And Maya scribes had the *write* stuff. They used up to 500 symbols, sort of like the hieroglyphics of ancient Egypt, to record important dates in history.

ON THE BALL

For fun, people across Maya lands went out to watch a game played with a rubber ball. The rules varied over time and in different areas, but the general idea was that teams passed the ball using their bodies to touch it but not their hands or feet. The game was played on a court made of plaster or dried mud. Sloped walls helped keep the ball in play, as teams tried to move the ball into what was like an end zone in modern American football.

The greatness of the Maya didn't last. Around 850, drought and other conditions led them to leave their cities. But they left behind ball courts and other buildings that people still explore today. And about six million Maya still live in Mexico and Central America.

COUNTING THE DAYS

Along with creating a writing system, the Maya developed several calendars. One had 365 days, like our modern calendar. But unlike our calendar year, the Maya Haab cycle was divided into 19 months, with one of them having just five days! Around 500 B.C.E., the Maya created a separate calendar for tracking religious events. It had 260 days and was related to the growing cycle of corn—its length generally matched the length of time a human baby spends inside their mother before they're born. A different calendar called the Long Count was used to keep track of historical events. Each cycle recorded on this calendar lasted more than 5,000 years! The first cycle began in what we know as 3114 B.C.E. Some of today's Maya still use these ancient calendars to mark the days and years.

THE AMERICAS 7TH CENTURY – 10TH CENTURY THE MAYA

47

The Wonders of CHICHÉN ITZÁ

Play Ball!

Need proof that the Maya really loved their ball game? Check out the court at Chichén Itzá. At 551 feet (168 m) long and 231 feet (70 m) wide, it's the largest one ever found. It's almost too large—one expert thinks it would have been hard to play the game on a court so big, so this one may have been more for show. The walls of the court have several stone rings that jut out. Sometimes the players passed the ball through the hoops, but that was not the object of the game (see page 47).

Holy Holes

The Maya at Chichén Itzá got much of their water from wells called cenotes. They believed that their rain god Chac lived in the cenotes, and they had to keep him happy to make sure they got enough rain. At cenotes across Maya lands, people dropped gifts into the wells, such as pottery. One gift left at a cenote at Chichén Itzá was a gold disk. Bones have been found at the bottom of some of the wells, so the Maya might have offered human sacrifices to Chac, too.

When most of the great Maya cities of the south began to crumble, one in Mexico's Yucatán region stood strong. Chichén Itzá was a home for the Maya and another people called the Toltecs from about the year 450 until about 1400. The city was a religious center, and traders brought goods there, too. Today, visitors can explore the remains of fine examples of Maya building skill.

The Temple of Kukulkan

This temple devoted to a Maya god is also known today as El Castillo—Spanish for "the Castle." Each side of this 79-foot (24-m)-high pyramid has 91 steps leading to the top; the platform there is one last step. That's 365 steps in all, to match the number of days in a year. Inside the pyramid was a throne covered with the gemstone jade.

Shadow of the Snake

Kukulkan was a god who took the shape of a snake. Maya builders placed the temple so that twice a year, on the spring and fall equinox, a shadow of a snake falls on the steps. The shadow seems to move down the staircase as the sun moves. When the shadow reaches the ground, it meets a stone serpent head placed at the base of the stairs.

Warriors Welcome

The Temple of the Warriors got its name from the images of warriors found on stone columns around the building. On the top of the temple is a statue called a Chac Mool. A Chac Mool is a reclining male figure, with his knees pulled up and head facing out. A bowl that may have been used to hold items offered during sacrifices to the gods sits on his stomach. Similar statues have been found all over Maya lands.

Scanning the Skies

When the Maya wanted to get a glimpse at the stars, they might have headed to El Caracol. In Spanish, *caracol* means "snail," and the winding stairs inside this building must have reminded someone of that tiny critter's spiral shell. The dome-shaped roof at the top of the building looks a little like the modern buildings where telescopes are kept. And it's likely the Maya climbed to the top of El Caracol to study the sky. From the windows, a Maya could track the position of Venus. The Maya used the planet's location as a guide for carrying out raids against their enemies.

MAJOR MOUNDS

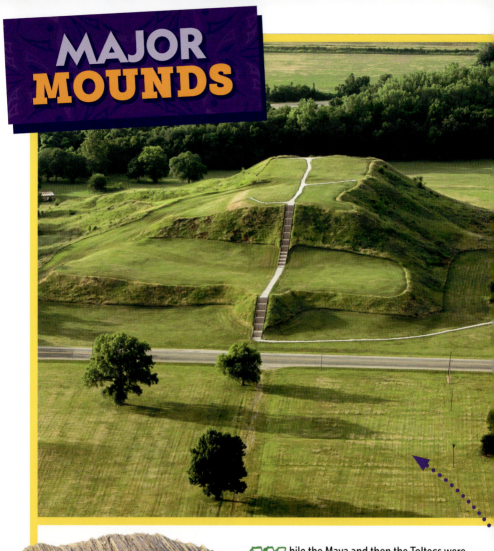

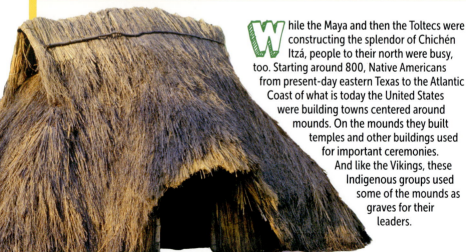

While the Maya and then the Toltecs were constructing the splendor of Chichén Itzá, people to their north were busy, too. Starting around 800, Native Americans from present-day eastern Texas to the Atlantic Coast of what is today the United States were building towns centered around mounds. On the mounds they built temples and other buildings used for important ceremonies. And like the Vikings, these Indigenous groups used some of the mounds as graves for their leaders.

WHO WERE THE MOUND BUILDERS?

A group of Indigenous people called the Caddo built some of the mounds that still dot the United States. But the major mound builders are known today as the Mississippians. Most of their towns were located along the Mississippi or other nearby rivers. The Mississippians started building their mound sites around 900. They were largely farmers, growing corn, though they also hunted for food and gathered wild nuts and berries.

The Mississippians were part of a large trade network. From the Great Lakes region, they got copper. Communities along the Gulf of Mexico and Atlantic Coast traded shells, which skilled Mississippian artists turned into cups and beads.

DURING THE **19TH CENTURY,** RESIDENTS OF **ST. LOUIS** DIDN'T KNOW THE IMPORTANCE OF THE **CAHOKIA MOUNDS,** AND THEY TOOK DIRT FROM THE MOUNDS FOR **BUILDING PROJECTS.**

THE GRAND CITY

If Chichén Itzá was the hot spot for the Maya, Cahokia was the center of Mississippian culture. It was located in what is now southern Illinois, near the border with St. Louis, Missouri. The site had up to 100 mounds, and a wooden wall made of logs up to 20 feet (6 m) tall guarded the heart of the city. Inside the wall, some of Cahokia's most important citizens lived on top of mounds. Getting around a mound wasn't always easy. Monks Mound, the largest, was 1,000 feet (305 m) around at its base, and the top towered 100 feet (30 m) above the city. It covered an area of about 14 acres (6 ha), and is the largest mound made by humans in North America.

Cahokia was a center of trade for the Mississippians, and at its peak, it had 5,000 or more people living in it. Thousands more lived outside the main city. By around 1200, though, people began to leave Cahokia, and experts aren't sure why. By the late 1300s, the city was empty.

MAKING A MOUND

What does it take to build something as large as Monks Mound? A whole lot of dirt! Mississippian builders dug up soil and carried it to the site in baskets—some 15 million basketfuls of soil. After the workers dumped out the dirt, they pressed it down with their feet. Then they headed out to get another load and do it all over again. Once a mound was finished, the Mississippians often put up buildings on its flat top. These were usually made out of wooden posts and had thatched roofs.

51

SPOTLIGHT: IN THE MOOD FOR FOOD

RICE IS NICE

Rice was a super crop for many medieval people, especially in Asia. It was domesticated about 8,000 years ago in China and slightly later in other parts of the world. The Prophet Muhammad was said to like rice, and Muslim traders may have taken the crop to North Africa and then Spain. Rice is a good grain, because its seeds are easy to store and move from place to place.

Here's a simple truth: Everybody needs food. For the Maya, Mississippians, and other great medieval civilizations, growing lots of food helped their populations grow. And if a small group of farmers could raise enough food for everyone, more people could take on other jobs, such as building tremendous temples or massive mounds. Here are some of the foods that fed the growth of medieval empires.

IN MEDIEVAL ITALY, SOME PEOPLE USED RICE AS A MEDICINE.

PEAS, PLEASE

In medieval Europe, peas played a big role on the table and on the farm. For peasants, peas were a common food: A good source of protein, they were often mixed with other vegetables. In England, peas were also called "pease"; there, yellow peas were used to make a pudding. Peas helped add nitrogen to the fields where they grew. This nutrient kept the soil healthy for growing a range of other crops.

A-MAIZE-ING CROP

There's nothing corny about it—the people of North and South America relied heavily on corn. In modern times in some parts of the world, it's called maize. Thousands of years ago, people in Mexico began to domesticate a wild grain called teosinte. That plant was the origin of today's corn. The Maya believed that one of their gods died in a battle with a demon and was reborn as a corn stalk. Today, more than one billion tons of corn are grown around the world each year!

GO FOR THE SORGHUM

No, it's not a kind of chewing gum. Sorghum is a grain that was first grown in East Africa more than 5,000 years ago. After spreading across Africa, sorghum was grown in Asia, too. What made sorghum good to grow? Well, for one thing, it could survive long periods without rain. And it's packed with nutrients. Farm animals like to eat it, too. Sorghum kernels can be popped, just like popcorn!

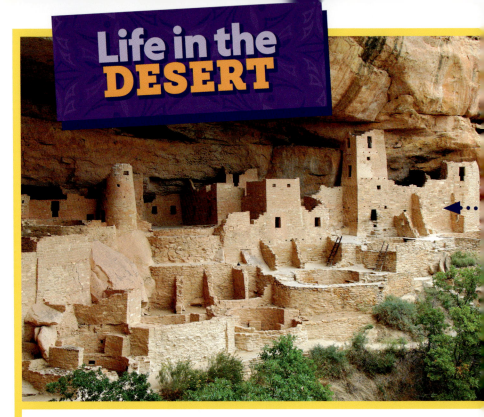

Life in the DESERT

How do you live in a desert? For the ancestors of today's Pueblo people, the answer was use water wisely and make your buildings out of adobe and stone. The ancient Pueblo people did a lot with a little and built a great civilization in what is now the Four Corners region of the United States. This is where the states of Arizona, Colorado, New Mexico, and Utah meet.

DESERT NEIGHBORS

The ancient Pueblo people weren't alone in this remote part of the desert Southwest. Other civilizations took root there, too, like the Mogollon, and the ancestors of several of today's Native American people, such as the Zuni and Hopi. All of these people relied on corn as a major food, though they raised beans, squash, and other crops, too. The people of the region also built clay pots for cooking and to store water and food. Keeping corn in the pots helped prevent it from rotting. But the pots weren't just kitchen dishes. Artists painted on them, depicting wildlife or geometric designs. Among the ancient Pueblo people, women were often the potters, and a mother passed on her favorite designs to her daughters.

SOME **ANCIENT PEOPLE OF THE SOUTHWEST** BUILT CANALS SEVERAL **HUNDRED MILES** LONG TO BRING **WATER** TO THEIR CROPS.

BIG BUILDINGS

Of all the desert dwellers, the ancient Pueblo people were the pros at constructing villages made of stone. Their premier site was Chaco Canyon in New Mexico. The ancient Pueblo people had already lived there for hundreds of years. Then, around 850, they began to build a cluster of buildings, using mud to hold rocks in place. The main buildings are called great houses. The largest at Chaco, called Pueblo Bonito, has 800 rooms! At Chaco Canyon's peak in the 11th century, about 5,000 people lived there.

Chaco was also a trading center. Roads led to the site from all directions, and the remains of goods the ancient Pueblo people got from Mexico and neighboring lands included copper bells, feathers from tropical birds, and chocolate.

A REAL CLIFF-HANGER

North of Chaco, in what is now Colorado, the Ancestral Puebloan people lived at Mesa Verde. They built their homes under cliffs that hung overhead. At first the homes were made of wood and mud, but then the Mesa Verdeans used stone, as in Chaco Canyon. Like the other Ancestral Puebloans, the people at Mesa Verde farmed, but they also hunted deer, rabbits, and other animals. All their tools were made of stone, bones, or wood.

During the 13th century, the people of Chaco and Mesa Verde left their stone towns. Why? Most likely because of a drought, but the people also might have been squabbling with each other. Today their buildings still stand, proof of this great desert civilization.

THE ROUND ROOMS

The ruins at Chaco and other Southwest sites have round rooms called kivas that were used for religious ceremonies and other important events. People entered them by going down a ladder that stuck out through a hole in the roof. Inside were benches and a pit for a fire. When the ancient Pueblo people left the region during the 13th century and headed deeper into what is now New Mexico, they took along the tradition of building kivas. The Pueblo people of New Mexico still use them today.

THE AMERICAS · 9TH CENTURY – 13TH CENTURY · ANCIENT PUEBLO PEOPLE

WHAT'S IN A WORD?

Anasazi

This word comes from a Navajo word that can mean "ancient ones." Historians and others once called the builders of Chaco Canyon Anasazi, but today the preferred term is Ancestral Puebloan or ancient Pueblo people, as Native Americans who live in villages called pueblos trace their roots to them.

CHACO RUINS

55

The Land of GOLD

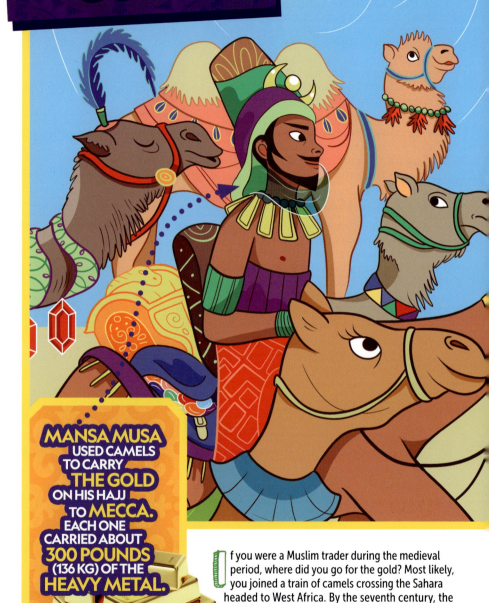

MANSA MUSA USED CAMELS TO CARRY **THE GOLD** ON HIS HAJJ TO **MECCA.** EACH ONE CARRIED ABOUT **300 POUNDS (136 KG)** OF THE **HEAVY METAL.**

If you were a Muslim trader during the medieval period, where did you go for the gold? Most likely, you joined a train of camels crossing the Sahara headed to West Africa. By the seventh century, the kingdom of Ghana was a budding center for trade in that part of Africa. When Muslim traders began coming there, they sought gold and ivory. Soon, they named Ghana "the land of gold."

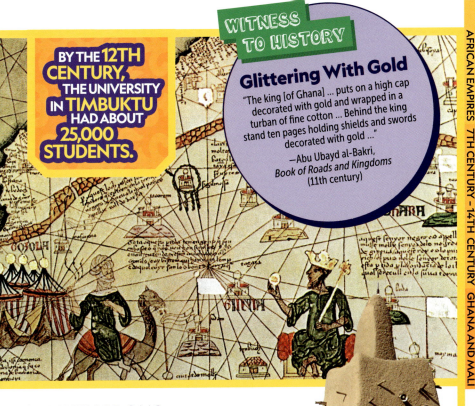

BY THE 12TH CENTURY, THE UNIVERSITY IN TIMBUKTU HAD ABOUT 25,000 STUDENTS.

WITNESS TO HISTORY
Glittering With Gold
"The king [of Ghana] ... puts on a high cap decorated with gold and wrapped in a turban of fine cotton ... Behind the king stand ten pages holding shields and swords decorated with gold ..."
—Abu Ubayd al-Bakri, *Book of Roads and Kingdoms* (11th century)

A VIEW OF TIMBUKTU

NEW KINGDOMS

As in the desert Southwest of what is now the United States, the area of Africa near the Niger and Senegal Rivers became home to several important civilizations. By the 11th century, Muslim traders were followed by Muslim raiders, who weakened Ghana's power. But within 200 years, another strong kingdom had risen in the region: Mali. The founder of Mali was a prince named Sundiata Keita, a name meaning "Lion Prince." After defeating a king named Sumanguru in 1235, Sundiata took over the old lands of Ghana and beyond. Under him and his son Mansa Uli, some members of the ruling class of the kingdom adopted Islam.

MAN-SA OF THE HOUR

Mali reached its peak under Mansa Musa, who ruled from 1312 into the 1330s. By then, Mali had become the world's second largest empire, after the Mongols (see pages 102–103). As it had been in Ghana, gold was still the main source of wealth, and Musa wasn't shy about showing it off. In 1324, when he went to Mecca, the holiest city in Islam, he brought with him several thousand people—and about a ton (0.9 t) of gold!

When Mali dominated West Africa, Mansa Musa used some of his great wealth to build a capital, Timbuktu. It became one of the great cities of the Middle Ages. Musa built a grand mosque there. He also built a palace and brought in Muslim scholars from Arab lands to teach there. The city became a center of Islamic learning, where scholars made copies of works first written in other Muslim lands.

AFRICAN EMPIRES 7TH CENTURY – 14TH CENTURY GHANA AND MALI

57

Find Your Place in MEDIEVAL EUROPE

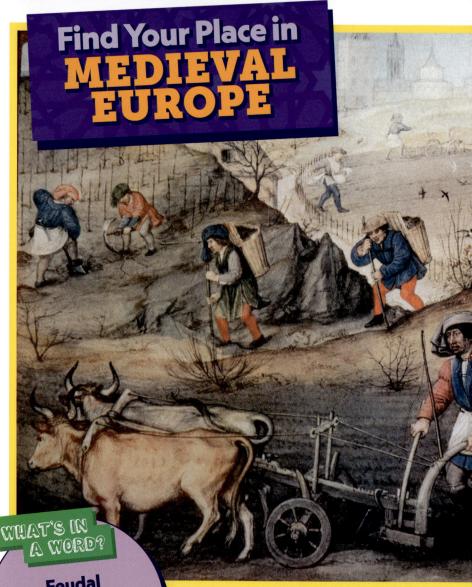

WHAT'S IN A WORD?

Feudal

"Feudal" and "feudalism" come from words coined by French historians in the 17th century. Their root is the Latin word *feudum*, which meant a grant of land, called a "fief" in English.

What was going on in parts of Europe while great civilizations were springing up around the world? Plenty—including the growth of a new kind of society. By the eighth century, it was clear that people fell into one of three broad categories. Most folks had to work the land to produce food. Another group was made up of monks, nuns, and priests—the people who prayed. And a small group of people ran the government and fought wars. Together, these three groups were at the heart of what's known today as feudalism.

FEUDAL FEUDS

How did this feudal society start, and what was it like? Well, if you want to start a hot debate among historians, these are good questions to ask! There are no easy answers, and views about feudalism have changed over time. It's not as if a few people got together and said, "Let's create feudalism." It developed over several centuries, and it could vary across different parts of Europe. But a few things were true. Feudalism provided some order after the collapse of the western Roman empire and the invasions of the fifth century. And people had defined roles in society. If you were born a peasant, odds were you'd stay a peasant. Also, if you were in the ruling class, you had things much easier than the people you ruled.

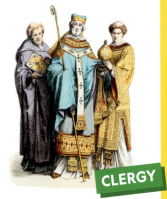
CLERGY

LAND AND LOYALTY

To get the lay of the feudal land, you must start with ... well, land. In the early part of the Middle Ages, land was a source of wealth. And people who owned a lot of it often wanted more. This could lead to wars, which meant small landowners lost what little they had. They and other people without land needed protection. The people who owned land, called lords, offered to provide this protection. In return, they wanted the "little people" with no money or land to farm for them. The lords ruled their lands like mini-kingdoms, though they had to be ready to serve the real king or queen when they needed help. The lord made an oath of fealty—their promise to come when the ruler called.

LORDS & LADIES

PEASANTS

Several rulers had a hand in shaping feudalism. One was Charlemagne (see pages 34–35). He gave away land to wealthy men to make sure they would fight for him. After feudalism was established in France during the ninth and 10th centuries, William the Conqueror brought it with him when he invaded England in the 11th century (see page 109). His eventual victory over the English resistance is called the Norman Conquest. After his victory, William said all the land was his. He then started giving it out to nobles called barons.

Where there's a Will there's a way.

Know Your Social Ranks

So, who were the feudal folks of medieval Europe? Here's a deeper look at the different groups, from the most to the least powerful.

KINGS AND QUEENS

At the top of the heap was the king or queen who ruled a kingdom. He or she sometimes claimed to be doing God's work on Earth, so no one should challenge them. The king or queen and their family members were called royalty. They could use their power to amass great wealth, but they were also expected to protect all the people they ruled. A king or queen ran the kingdom from a place called their court, and the people who directly served the ruler were also called a court.

NOBLES

A noble who took land from a king in exchange for fighting for him during wartime was called a vassal. Nobles came in different ranks. Under a system that began in France, they included dukes, earls, and barons. The land a noble received was called a fief, and he could give some of that away and choose his own vassals. To the nobles, the king was their lord. But how much military aid they gave to their lord varied. In some cases, a noble could send a knight who owed him fealty to take his place in battle. Nobles could usually pass on their fiefs to their relatives. And some medieval folk could reach the rank of noble as merchants—they bought and sold the goods others made. See pages 144–145 for more on merchants.

WITNESS TO HISTORY

A Promise

"I will ... be true and faithful and love all which he loves and shun all which he shuns, according to the laws of God and the order of the world. Nor will I ever with will or action, through word or deed, do anything which is unpleasing to him."

—Anglo-Saxon oath of fealty

KNIGHTS

Knights were often vassals of the nobility. They might have come from poor families, but they had enough money to equip themselves for battle and learned military skills. Like a noble, a knight had to be ready to fight when called by his lord. But in the later Middle Ages, some knights got out of that promise by giving the noble money.

SERFS AND PEASANTS

You may be wondering who was keeping the fiefs running if knights were serving nobles and nobles were serving kings. The dirty work went to peasants and serfs. Was it pleasant being a peasant? Not really. Peasants were poor and had to work hard, but at least they could move freely from one place to another. Not so for serfs: A serf couldn't leave the land they farmed for their lord—called a manor—unless the lord said so. Serfs spent part of their time working the manor for the lord. Then they could farm whatever small piece of land on the manor the lord gave them—but they had to turn over a share of the food they raised there. And serfs weren't just farmers. They also had to care for any bridges and roads on the lord's manor.

SHOGUNS and Samurai

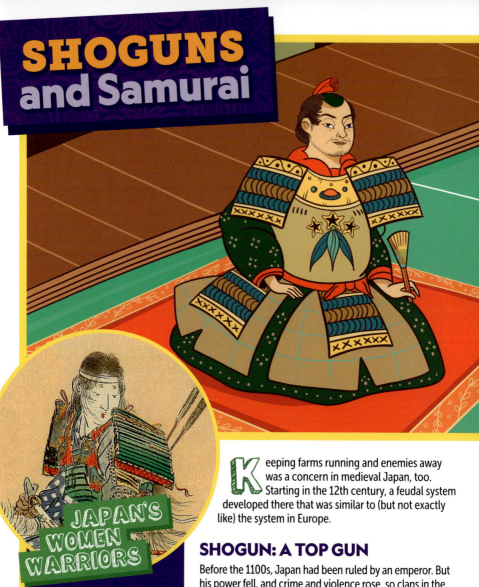

JAPAN'S WOMEN WARRIORS

The samurai weren't the only trained fighters in Japan. Often their daughters learned the same fighting skills. These female samurai were called *onna bugeisha*. They often defended the family's home or village from enemy attack. But one of these women warriors really made her mark on the battlefield. Tomoe Gozen fought for the shogun Yoshinaka. She could handle both a bow and a sword, and an ancient Japanese text said she defeated some of the fiercest enemy troops.

Keeping farms running and enemies away was a concern in medieval Japan, too. Starting in the 12th century, a feudal system developed there that was similar to (but not exactly like) the system in Europe.

SHOGUN: A TOP GUN

Before the 1100s, Japan had been ruled by an emperor. But his power fell, and crime and violence rose, so clans in the countryside banded together for safety. Two of these clans clashed in 1185, and the Minamoto came out on top. The clan's leader, Yoritomo, became the shogun, or military dictator. There was still an emperor, but Yoritomo and the shoguns who followed him were the real bosses of Japan.

Just as the kings and lords of Europe needed help fighting wars, so did the shoguns. So they gave land to loyal men who served them. In return, these men were like the vassals of Europe and had to provide soldiers to the shoguns. The vassals felt a close tie to their lords, sometimes even referring to them as parents. They often hired jitō, or land stewards, to run their estates, and either a man or a woman could hold the job.

MEDIEVAL ASIA 12TH CENTURY FEUDAL JAPAN

IN A SPORT CALLED **NIKKO**, BASED ON **SAMURAI TRAINING,** THE PARTICIPANTS FIRED **ARROWS** AT WOODEN TARGETS WHILE **RIDING AT FULL SPEED.**

EYE ON THE SAMURAI

Often, the landowners or the people who ran their lands hired the services of highly skilled warriors called samurai. The name means "ones who serve." They came from the upper classes of Japanese society. Along with fierce loyalty to their lords, the samurai believed in a code of honor, called the Bushido. A samurai who was captured in battle killed himself, rather than accept defeat. On the other side, winning samurai might chop off the head of an enemy soldier. Then, the head was presented as a gift to their generals.

The earliest samurai used bows and arrows and fought on horseback. After foreign invasions in the 13th century, these warriors began using swords more often, fighting in hand-to-hand combat. Samurai started to train at an early age, and a few became the sly spies called ninjas. Ninjas had been around for centuries and were highly skilled in martial arts.

63

The SAMURIGHT STUFF

SWORDS

Let's cut to the chase: A samurai knew how to use a sword—or four. A samurai had a long, slightly curved sword called a *katana* that he swung using two hands. Another long sword was called a *tachi*. Samurai also had shorter sword called a *wakizashi* and an even shorter blade called a *tanto*.

NAGINATA

A *naginata* was another deadly samurai weapon. It featured a short, curved blade attached to a long pole. A samurai often used it to slice at the legs of an enemy soldier's horse. When the horse went down, the naginata was used to kill the rider.

WAR FAN

Some samurai were fans of fans. But these weren't fans for keeping them cool. Officers used them to signal their troops. Some were made of lacquered paper, but others were a lot tougher. They were made of metal blades, so they could also serve as small shields.

BOW AND ARROW

Early samurai fought mostly on horseback, and bows and arrows were their main weapon. The bow, called a *yumi*, was about seven feet (2 m) long. Because of the size of the bow and the armor they wore, samurai did not shoot as they rode—they came to a stop first.

64

Here's a look at how a typical samurai suited up for battle.

HELMET

Samurai had to keep their head—that is, stay calm during battle. But they also wanted to keep their actual head, so each wore a helmet called a *kabuto*. Besides covering a samurai's head, a kabuto had a piece attached to the back of the helmet that protected his neck. The neck guard might be made of strips of iron or leather covered with lacquer, which is made from tree sap and hardens as it dries. The horns often found on kabutos helped fellow soldiers locate a samurai during the heat of battle—and could be a little scary to the enemy, too. Some helmets also included a face mask. You might recognize a samurai helmet on a familiar movie villain: The helmet worn by Darth Vader in the *Star Wars* movies was based on them.

ARMOR

Like the neck guard, samurai armor was made up of small pieces of lacquered iron or leather. The strips were tied together with pieces of silk thread. The armor included guards to protect the thighs and a large piece to protect the upper body. Shoulder guards were meant to shield against enemy arrows. Another guard protected the arm the samurai used to hold his bow. Samurai who fought on foot wore lighter armor than those who rode a horse because they needed to be able to move quickly on the battlefield. Some armor had images such as dragons painted on them.

An INDIAN Empire

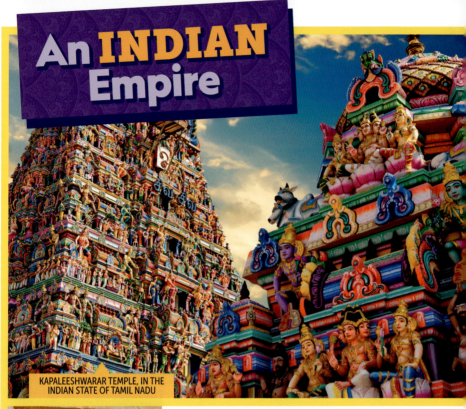

KAPALEESHWARAR TEMPLE, IN THE INDIAN STATE OF TAMIL NADU

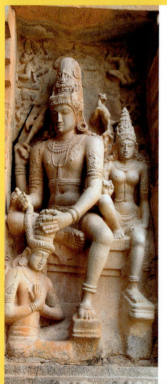

Asia was a busy place during the Middle Ages. Over the centuries, the world's largest continent saw empires rise and fall. One that rose, and kept rising for a long time, was the Chola of southern India.

RISING TO THE TOP

Kings connected to the Chola family ruled as far back as the second century B.C.E. The Chola were one of three powerful families in the part of southern India now called Tamil Nadu. During the ninth and 10th centuries, the Cholas went to war and defeated the other two families. They created a dynasty that ruled for about 400 years. Through conquest, they gained territory up and down the eastern coast of India. One Chola king, Rajendra, also took his troops inland and defeated several foes. He then took water from the Ganges, a sacred river in India, and brought it home as a sign of his victory. The Cholas also used politics to spread their influence even further. By giving gifts to local rulers, they won the rulers' loyalty. At the dynasty's peak, the Cholas controlled the island of Sri Lanka and smaller islands. Their influence reached what is now Malaysia, about 1,500 miles (2,414 km) away, and Chola diplomats visited China.

RUNNING AN EMPIRE

Along with being skilled fighters, the Cholas knew how to keep their empire humming. They chose local officials to handle local government issues, but they made sure everyone knew the Cholas were in charge. They did this in part by building huge temples to honor the Hindu gods. Hinduism was and remains the main religion of India. The temples served to link the kings to the gods, so the people would respect the kings. A 10th-century Chola queen named Sembiyan Mahadevi built large stone temples, and members of the dynasty that followed built even grander ones.

MAKING MONEY AND ART

While many people of the empire farmed, traders exchanged goods such as cotton, silks, spices, and jewels with merchants from other lands. Some citizens were great artists. They created paintings and carved beautiful stone sculptures to decorate the empire's temples. Chola bronze workers were especially skilled in making statues. They poured the liquid metal into molds made of wax and surrounded by clay. When heated, the wax melted, leaving the clay mold and the sculpture.

HONORING THE DANCING GOD

Hinduism has many gods, and the most important for the Chola rulers was Shiva. One of the three major Hindu gods, Shiva is considered a god capable of both creation and destruction. In his form of Shiva Nataraja, he is "lord of the dance." Chola artists created sculptures of the dancing god, and temples were built to honor him.

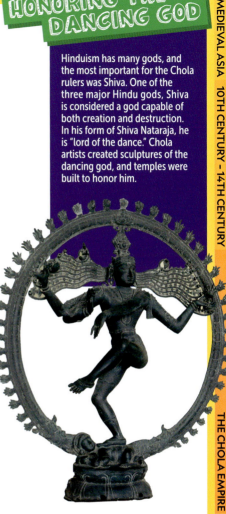

MEDIEVAL ASIA | 10TH CENTURY - 14TH CENTURY | THE CHOLA EMPIRE

THE **WATER** TAKEN FROM THE **GANGES** WAS BROUGHT TO A **NEWLY** BUILT CITY CALLED **GANGAIKOND-ACHOLAPURAM**, WHICH MEANS "THE **CITY** TO WHICH THE **CHOLA EMPEROR** BROUGHT THE GANGES."

Rah Rah for RAJARAJA

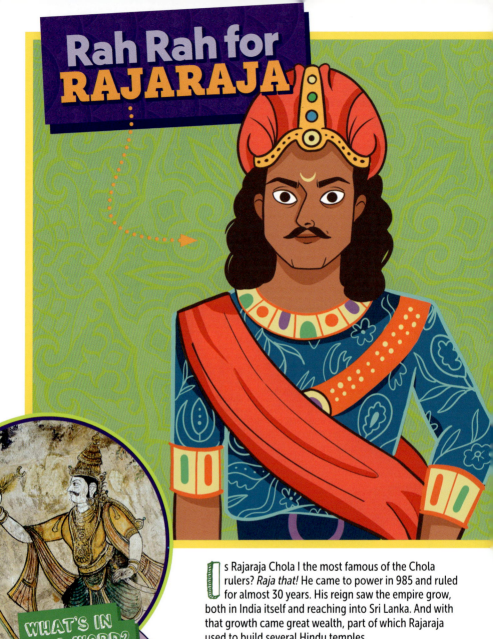

WHAT'S IN A WORD?

Raja
"Raja" comes from a Sanskrit word meaning "king," so Rajaraja was "king king."

Is Rajaraja Chola I the most famous of the Chola rulers? *Raja that!* He came to power in 985 and ruled for almost 30 years. His reign saw the empire grow, both in India itself and reaching into Sri Lanka. And with that growth came great wealth, part of which Rajaraja used to build several Hindu temples.

A WARRIOR KING

Even before taking the throne, Rajaraja was known as an excellent fighter. During his first years as king, he strengthened his army. Then he set out to attack enemy kingdoms. His son Rajendra sometimes fought next to his father in these wars. In one case, Rajaraja couldn't defeat the kingdom of Vengi on the battlefield. So, he arranged for a marriage between his daughter and a Vengi prince,

WITNESS TO HISTORY

Rajaraja's Victories

"In his life of growing strength ... he was pleased to destroy ships (at) Kandalur-Śalai, and conquered by his army, which was victorious in great battles ..."

—Inscription on a Thanjavur Temple

creating a strong link between the kingdoms. Rajaraja also had a skilled navy, which he used to bring troops to Sri Lanka and capture smaller islands called the Maldives. Unlike other kings before him, Rajaraja recorded details of his military victories. He used writings called inscriptions carved into temple walls.

READY TO RULE

Rajaraja, though, was more than a fighter. From his capital of Thanjavur, he set up a detailed system for collecting taxes. He also chose local government officials and gave them a lot of freedom to run their own affairs. But Rajaraja still kept an eye on how the money was spent. And although he was a devout follower of Shiva, the king let his people worship other gods. He also allowed the building of a Buddhist temple. That religion had been founded in India about 1,500 years before Rajaraja's reign.

Rajaraja showed his own faith by building the Brihadishvara Temple in Thanjavur. At the time, it was India's largest Hindu temple. Construction took about six years. The granite temple was completed around 1010, just a few years before Rajaraja died. Its main tower soars to a height of just over 196 feet (60 m). Outside the temple was a fort with a moat around it, similar to many medieval European castles.

When Rajaraja's son Rajendra became king, he continued some of his father's ways. Like Rajaraja, Rajendra won many battlefield victories and expanded the empire. He also built an even larger temple with the same name as his father's.

INSIDE A CHOLA TEMPLE

The temples built by Rajaraja and other Chola kings were places of worship—and sometimes much more. At the temples, poor residents of the empire could win respect from those in higher social classes by donating items such as lamps or flowers. Merchants and others with more money could show off their wealth and status by donating jewelry or silk. Their gifts might also show their support for the king, since he had built the temple. The money the temples took in was used to provide jobs for local people. And at times the temples were even local banks, loaning money—for a fee.

MEDIEVAL ASIA 947 - 1014 RAJARAJA

69

STRONG SONG

India's neighbor to the north saw a great empire rise during the Middle Ages. China had been ruled by royal dynasties for centuries, going back to about 1770 B.C.E. By the early 900s, though, the country was divided into different territories under the command of competing warlords. One of these men was Chao K'uang-yin. In 960, he was able to defeat his rivals and reunite most of China. He founded the Song dynasty.

HITTING THE RIGHT NOTES

As the new emperor, Chao K'uang-yin went right to work. He replaced military governors with officials he chose himself and assumed command of the army. After Chao K'uang-yin died in 976, his brother Taizong took over the dynasty. He hired even more educated men to run things. The economy did well, too. Farmers in the southern part of the empire raised plenty of crops, including tea and a new kind of rice. It grew fast enough for farmers to plant two crops of it a year. Boats traveled the Grand Canal to bring the rice to other parts of China. With more food available, China's population exploded, and cities grew. The city of Hangzhou became a center of trade and business. For a time, it was the Song capital, and its population reached more than one million.

Song rulers stressed education, starting with government officials. The arts thrived, too. Potters made items out of porcelain, sculptors worked with metal, and painters created images on silk and paper. Meanwhile, Song architects designed buildings called pagodas that could be more than 300 feet (91 m) tall.

THE SONG AT SEA

Under the Song, the Chinese knew something *aboat* sailing. Merchant ships traveled on rivers and oceans to trade with foreign countries as far away as the Persian Gulf. Some ships were powered by paddle wheels, with men on treadmills running in place to make the wheels turn. Shipbuilders added rudders to the rear of vessels to make them easier to steer. Song rulers also created China's first permanent navy—the largest in the world at that time. Some larger warships had catapults that could shoot firebombs at the enemy.

SO LONG, SONG

Of course, the Song dynasty hit some sour notes along the way, too. Wealthy landowners got greedy and raised the rents they charged peasant farmers. This led the peasants to sometimes rebel. And the Song rulers and government officials shrank the military, so the empire could not defend itself well. Tribes to the north invaded in the early 12th century and started their own dynasty on Song lands. A new Song dynasty survived in the south, but it couldn't stop the Mongols from taking over the country in 1279 (see pages 102–103).

TEA SUITED SONG EMPEROR HUIZONG TO A T—HE WROTE A BOOK EXPLAINING HOW TO GROW THE TEA PLANT AND HOW TO BREW A PERFECT CUP.

MEDIEVAL ASIA 960 - 1279 THE SONG DYNASTY

SPOTLIGHT: SONG SMARTS

Part of what made the Song dynasty so strong were the great inventions the residents of the empire came up with. And they weren't just good for the Middle Ages—we still use most of them today. Here's a look at some of these lasting inventions.

GUNPOWDER

The fireworks displays that make you ooh and aah are thanks to Song scientists. One of them found out how to mix the right chemicals to create gunpowder—the mixture that powers fireworks into the sky and makes them explode. As the story goes, the scientist was looking to create a mixture that would let him live forever. While that effort may have gone up in smoke, the fact is that by 1044, a Song military book explained how to make gunpowder and how to use it. The Chinese did make fireworks with the powder, but they also used it in weapons such as bombs and mines.

MOVABLE TYPE

When it came to printing on paper, the Chinese before the Song had already made a good impression. Buddhist monks dipped carved blocks of wood in ink. The blocks had entire sections of writing carved into them. The monks then pressed the inked blocks onto paper. One of the earliest books printed this way was made in 868. But under the Song, an inventor named Bi Sheng introduced what's called movable type. He made clay blocks for hundreds of characters used to write the Chinese language. Printing with this type of type made bookmaking go much faster. In 1313, the clay blocks were replaced with wood, and the number of individual characters reached the thousands.

MAGNETIC COMPASS

Long before GPS helped us get where we're going, travelers relied on compasses to find their way. A magnetic needle points north, so people can find it and the other three main directions. Around 1050, a Song scientist wrote about a magnetic compass, which was the first written record of the device. Even before then, the Chinese used a magnetic mineral called lodestone to make a spoon whose handle pointed south. It was the Song magnetic compass that guided travelers along their way. They were particularly useful for sailors at sea where landmarks were hard to come by.

PAPER MONEY

The Chinese introduced the first form of paper money during the ninth century, during the Tang dynasty. But it was the Song dynasty that papered China with bills, to replace the much heavier metal coins used as money. This was the world's first paper money issued by a government.

CANNONS AND ROCKETS

After they had gunpowder, the Song fired up two new weapons that used the explosive mix. A drawing from about 1127 shows what is probably the world's first cannon. Certainly, by the end of the Song dynasty, the Chinese had more of these big guns. The cannon took about two hundred years after that to reach Europe.

The first recorded use of Song rockets in battle comes from 1232. The rockets were called fire-arrows. A tube filled with gunpowder was attached to a stick. The bottom end of the tube was open, so escaping gas and smoke propelled the rocket forward. The stick helped the rocket fly straight once it took off.

A World of BELIEFS

During the Middle Ages, people believed in a wide range of gods and spirits. The mere mortals thought that these spiritual forces shaped their daily life—or an afterlife that might be waiting for them. Here's a look at where some of the world's major religions started.

Pagan Beliefs

To early Christians, anyone who did not accept their faith was a pagan, or nonbeliever. In Europe, these included the first Vikings of Scandinavia. They believed in many gods and goddesses. At the top was Odin, along with his son, Thor, the thunder god. A companion of theirs was Loki, who was known as a trickster god. One of Loki's daughters was Hel, the goddess of death.

Judaism

About 4,000 years ago, while their neighbors often worshipped several gods, people of the Middle East known as the Israelites were different. They said there was only one true God, and to him, they were a chosen people—God would protect them, if they followed his commands. Their religion became Judaism. By the Middle Ages, the followers of Judaism had spread across parts of Asia, North Africa, and Europe. They often faced prejudice because of their beliefs.

NORTH AMERICA

ATLANTIC OCEAN

PACIFIC OCEAN

SOUTH AMERICA

MAP KEY
■ Area of interest
Present-day countries are shown.

Christianity

Largely because of Constantine the Great's efforts (see page 11), Christianity became the main religion across the Roman and Byzantine Empires. But it got its start at the beginning of the first century C.E. in what is now Israel. The followers of a local Jewish spiritual leader named Jesus wrote down his teachings. These included the belief that he was the son of God—the same God the Israelites worshipped.

Animism

Across most of the medieval world, many people did not practice a formal religion. Their beliefs are today called animism. People in animistic regions, including Africa, parts of Asia, and the Americas, believed that everything on Earth has a soul or spirit—from rocks to rain and all living things. These unseen spirits shape such events as the weather and can cause sickness in people.

74

Islam

The teachings of the Prophet Muhammad led to the creation of Islam, another faith that worshipped the one God of the Jews and Christians. In Islam, God's name is Allah. During the Middle Ages, Islam spread from its birthplace in modern-day Saudi Arabia across parts of Asia, Africa, and Europe. Some of the great empires of the era were ruled by Muslims. And some of the greatest thinkers of the time also practiced Islam (see pages 28–29).

Hinduism

Hinduism developed in India more than 4,000 years ago. Its followers believe in many gods. The most important are Shiva (see page 67), Vishnu, and Brahma. Hindus believe in reincarnation, meaning that after a person dies, they are reborn as something or someone else—it could be as an animal or as a different person. This gives them the opportunity to do something they wanted to do in their old life but couldn't. It also gives them a chance to lead a more spiritual life. The goal is to follow Hindu teachings so well that a person stops dying and being reborn. A person's soul no longer experiences the pain of death. Achieving this is called reaching nirvana.

Buddhism

Like Islam, Buddhism had a single founder. A Hindu prince named Siddhartha Gautama was born in India around 560 B.C.E. Siddhartha saw great suffering all around him. He realized that humans could end their suffering, in part, by meditating and by following his teachings on the best way to live. This included not telling lies or speaking badly of others and not causing harm to any living things. His goal was to reach enlightenment—a state that ends the cycle of reincarnation. When Siddhartha reached this state, he was called the Buddha—the enlightened one. Although the Buddha developed his religion in India, by the Middle Ages it had spread across large parts of East Asia.

The CRUSADES

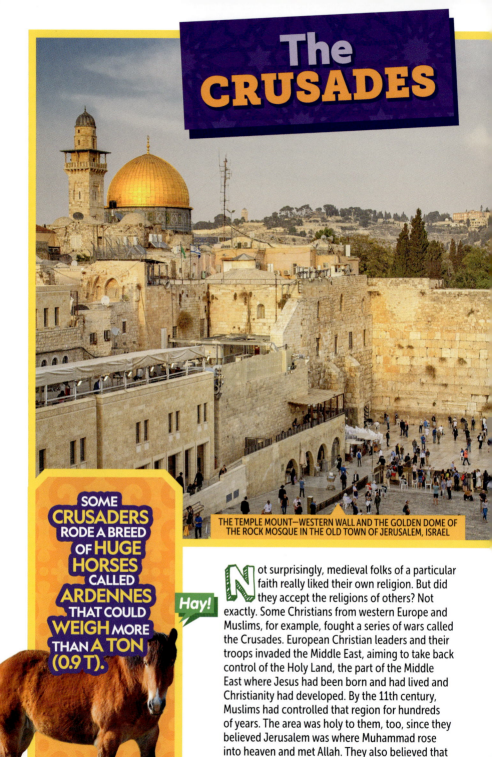

THE TEMPLE MOUNT—WESTERN WALL AND THE GOLDEN DOME OF THE ROCK MOSQUE IN THE OLD TOWN OF JERUSALEM, ISRAEL

SOME **CRUSADERS** RODE A BREED OF **HUGE HORSES** CALLED **ARDENNES** THAT COULD **WEIGH** MORE THAN **A TON** (0.9 T).

Hay!

Not surprisingly, medieval folks of a particular faith really liked their own religion. But did they accept the religions of others? Not exactly. Some Christians from western Europe and Muslims, for example, fought a series of wars called the Crusades. European Christian leaders and their troops invaded the Middle East, aiming to take back control of the Holy Land, the part of the Middle East where Jesus had been born and had lived and Christianity had developed. By the 11th century, Muslims had controlled that region for hundreds of years. The area was holy to them, too, since they believed Jerusalem was where Muhammad rose into heaven and met Allah. They also believed that Jesus was another of Allah's prophets.

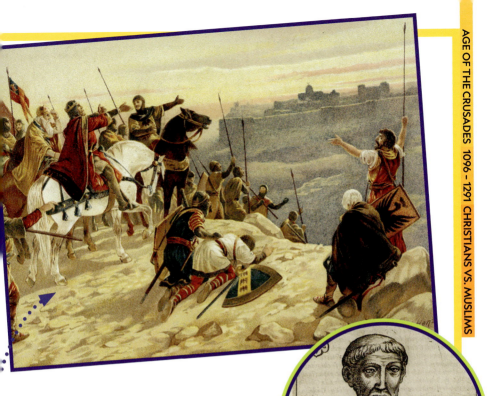

AGE OF THE CRUSADES 1096 - 1291 CHRISTIANS VS. MUSLIMS

THE FIRST CRUSADE

During the 11th century, an Islamic Turkic people called the Seljuks had seized part of the Byzantine Empire. Byzantine emperor Alexius asked for Pope Urban II's help in driving out the Muslims. The pope agreed, for several reasons. If Roman Catholic forces defeated the Turks, it would make Urban look good in Europe. A victory would also improve relations between the pope and Alexius. And maybe, just maybe, military success against the Turks would pave the way for Christians to take back the Holy Land.

INTO BATTLE

Under Urban's orders, a Christian force of about 100,000 knights set off for battle in 1096. Their first main target was the city of Antioch, in Syria. The knights defeated the Seljuks and then headed for Jerusalem with a much smaller force. They built towers and ladders of wood so they could get over the city's walls. Once inside, the Crusaders killed tens of thousands of Muslims.

With each of their victories, the Christian knights set up small states within the Muslim lands of the Middle East. But since this was called the First Crusade, you know there was a lot more fighting to come.

THE RECONQUEST

Before the First Crusade began, Catholic rulers in northern Spain began to fight Muslims who had taken over Spanish lands to the south. This marked the first major clash between Christians and Muslims in Europe since the eighth century. The Spanish efforts are known in English as the Reconquest. It took more than 400 years for the Spanish to complete the Reconquest. But their first military efforts during the 11th century convinced Pope Urban II to challenge the Muslims in the Holy Land.

77

CRUSADERS in CONTROL

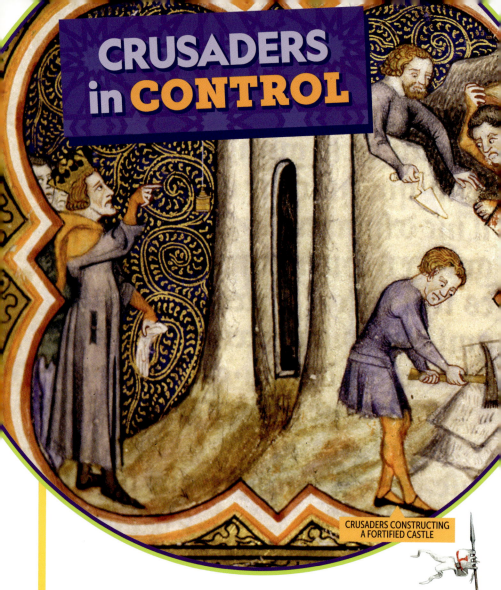

CRUSADERS CONSTRUCTING A FORTIFIED CASTLE

CHRISTIAN CRUSADERS SOMETIMES WENT INTO BATTLE SHOUTING DEUS VULT!—LATIN FOR "GOD WILLS IT."

The Roman Catholic knights didn't stop after their victory in Jerusalem. The Crusaders now controlled three small states, as they had already captured Antioch and Edessa. They would go on to take a fourth state, Tripoli, along with smaller cities. Most of the rulers of the four new states were from France, so the lands they controlled were called Frankish states. They were largely located in what are now Israel, Syria, Turkey, and Lebanon.

HARSH RULE

Let's be frank: The Frankish rulers could be cruel. They sometimes kept up their violent ways after the battles ended, killing Muslim civilians. They also killed Jews. Many medieval European Christians were prejudiced against Jews, and attacks on them went on in Europe, too. In Jerusalem, Christians, Muslims, and Jews had lived peacefully together under Islamic rule. But the Crusaders put an end to that, driving Jews and Muslims out of the city. The Franks also insulted the Muslims by putting a large Christian cross on top of a holy Islamic site, the Dome of the Rock. Eventually, though, the Franks let some Muslims and Jews back into Jerusalem. Some came to pray, others to work.

LIFE IN THE FRANKISH STATES

Franks poured into Jerusalem and the surrounding area and made up more than half the population. But in the other major cities, the outsiders were outnumbered by Greek Orthodox Christians. They had lived in the region from when it was under Byzantine control. Some Frankish nobles married into important Orthodox families.

Many goods came into the Frankish kingdom by sea, on Italian ships. Italy at the time had several independent cities with strong navies. These fleets helped the Franks take control of ports, and in return, the Italians got to control parts of the port cities and make money off the international trade. People came through the ports, too. The Franks needed the skills of such people as builders, armorers, and doctors.

PILGRIMS TO THE HOLY LAND

Even before the Crusades, pilgrims had set off for Jerusalem. No, not those guys in tall hats who landed on Plymouth Rock. Medieval pilgrims were people who left their home and made long journeys to important religious sites. They made these pilgrimages for different reasons. Some were trying to show their faith: Catholics, for example, might seek forgiveness for a sin. (Pope Urban II said that the Catholics who went on the First Crusade had all their sins forgiven.) For European peasants, the trips gave them a chance to explore the world outside their villages. And some came back with little souvenirs showing where they had been. Visitors to Jerusalem often brought home a small tin badge with a symbol of the city—a palm leaf. Other shrines had their own metal medals.

AGE OF THE CRUSADES 1096 - 1291 THE FRANKISH STATES

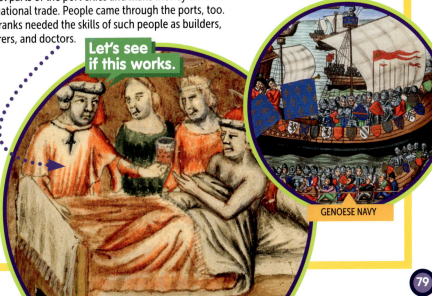

Let's see if this works.

GENOESE NAVY

79

What to WEAR TO WAR

A CHAIN MAIL SUIT COULD HAVE 200,000 METAL RINGS.

Crusaders and other warriors of this time needed to protect themselves from swords, arrows, and lances. How'd they do it? By suiting up in armor. Here's a look at what knights wore to protect themselves from enemy blows.

Shield

Metal suits weren't always enough, so knights also carried shields to protect them in combat. Wood, metal, and leather were all used to make shields. Shield size tended to shrink as the armor knights wore improved. Knights often painted their shields with certain colors or symbols to show who they fought for.

SHIELDS COULD DO MORE THAN JUST PROTECT. SOME GERMAN FIGHTERS USED THEIR SHIELDS TO CARRY A VICTORIOUS GENERAL OFF THE BATTLEFIELD.

"I should have gone before I left the house."

Chain Mail

For many knights, the check against swords was in the mail ... the chain mail. Chain mail was a flexible suit made from little rings of metal joined together. It usually covered the top of a knight's body, though some warriors wore much longer mail suits—and chain mail hoods, too. A chain mail suit could weigh up to 30 pounds (14 kg).

Metal Plates

By the 14th century, chain mail had lost its appeal. The creation of more powerful bows meant an archer's arrow could pierce the suit. This led knights to turn back to the past, and they began to use plates of solid metal tied together. (The invaders of the late Roman era had worn similar suits.)

Padding

Underneath their armor, knights wore padded cloth. This cloth kept the metal from rubbing knights the wrong way and hurting their skin. It also added another layer of protection against an enemy's hack or stab.

Armor Suits

Even the plates were not always good enough, so some knights went to the full metal suit. From head to toe, the knight was covered in steel that could weigh up to 55 pounds (25 kg). Some armor makers covered the steel with tin, to keep it from rusting. Once knights suited up, getting out again wasn't easy, so the suits had small flaps or trap doors for bathroom breaks. That way, a knight could relieve himself without taking off his gear.

Helmet

Topping off the suit of armor was head gear of some kind. Solid metal helmets replaced chain mail hoods during the Crusades. Some helmets had visors that slid down to protect the face. Later helmets featured horns and animals as decorations.

HORSES SOMETIMES HAD THEIR OWN ARMOR MADE FROM MAIL OR METAL PLATES.

81

A CRUSADING FAMILY

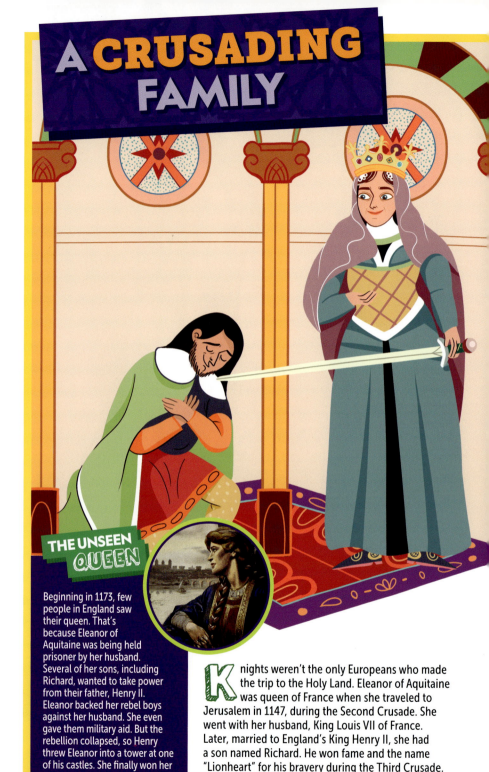

THE UNSEEN QUEEN

Beginning in 1173, few people in England saw their queen. That's because Eleanor of Aquitaine was being held prisoner by her husband. Several of her sons, including Richard, wanted to take power from their father, Henry II. Eleanor backed her rebel boys against her husband. She even gave them military aid. But the rebellion collapsed, so Henry threw Eleanor into a tower at one of his castles. She finally won her freedom after he died, in 1189.

Knights weren't the only Europeans who made the trip to the Holy Land. Eleanor of Aquitaine was queen of France when she traveled to Jerusalem in 1147, during the Second Crusade. She went with her husband, King Louis VII of France. Later, married to England's King Henry II, she had a son named Richard. He won fame and the name "Lionheart" for his bravery during the Third Crusade.

REALLY ROYAL

With her father's death in 1137, Eleanor had become the duchess of Aquitaine, an independent region in what is now France. She was just 15 when she took control of this important piece of property, which was larger than the kingdom of France. She became a queen for the first time the same year, when she married Louis. After her marriage to him ended, she married Henry, who became king of England. Two of her sons would later hold this title.

Eleanor was smart, and she took a keen interest in the politics of France and England. She's considered one of the most powerful women of the Middle Ages, as she helped run England while still watching over her own lands in Aquitaine.

THE CRUSADING SON

Richard I became king of England in 1189, though he spent most of his time in France, and—no *lion*—spoke almost no English. He was more interested in fighting in the Holy Land than ruling. To get money for battle, he once joked he would sell London if he could find someone rich enough to buy it. He reached the Holy Land in 1191 and battled the great Muslim ruler Saladin (see pages 92–93). Returning home, Richard was taken prisoner by an Austrian duke whom Richard had earlier insulted. Mom came to the rescue, paying a huge ransom to see her son released. Richard died in 1199 from a war injury.

RICHARD BECAME A SORT OF **BOGEYMAN** IN THE HOLY LAND. MUSLIM MOTHERS TOLD THEIR CHILDREN HE WOULD **GET THEM** IF THEY **MISBEHAVED!**

SPECIAL ORDERS

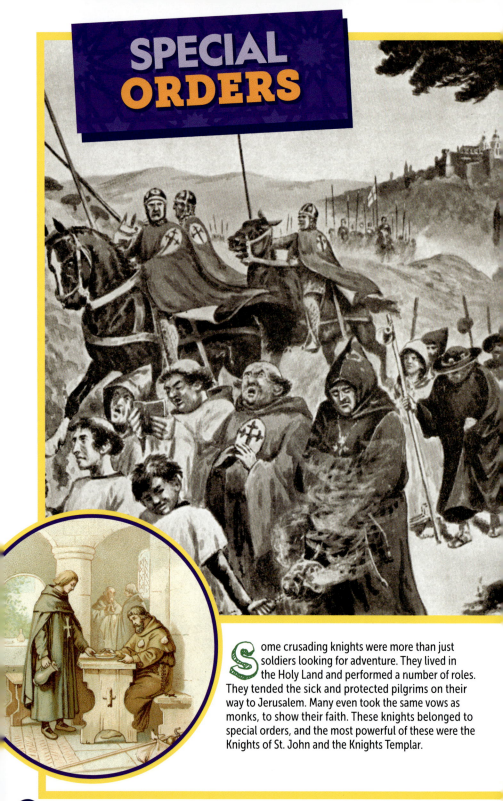

Some crusading knights were more than just soldiers looking for adventure. They lived in the Holy Land and performed a number of roles. They tended the sick and protected pilgrims on their way to Jerusalem. Many even took the same vows as monks, to show their faith. These knights belonged to special orders, and the most powerful of these were the Knights of St. John and the Knights Templar.

A CRACKERJACK CASTLE

Krak de Chevaliers, in Syria, has been called the most perfect medieval castle. It's certainly the best surviving example of a crusaders' castle, with some walls up to 80 feet (24 m) thick. When the Hospitallers were there, it was like a little city behind thick stone walls. Some 2,000 people could live in the castle for several years. Along with the knights and their horses, the castle was home to their squires, other soldiers, and workers who kept things humming. Storerooms held supplies of grain, and the knights even had a windmill to grind it.

FIGHTING MONKS

The Knights of St. John formed in Jerusalem several decades before the Crusades began. A group of monks ran a hospital there to take care of Christian pilgrims. After the First Crusade, the monks took on a military role, as well. These religious knights were called Hospitallers, because of their ties to the Jerusalem hospital.

NO HASSLES WITH CASTLES

In 1136, the Christian king of Jerusalem gave the Hospitallers, or Knights of St. John, a castle to defend. Several years later, the ruler of the Frankish state of Tripoli gave the order another castle, called the Krak de Chevaliers. It became the headquarters of the Hospitallers. They expanded it and strengthened it, as they did with other castles they took over. At one point, the Knights of St. John had about two dozen castles. They also stayed true to their medical roots, building hospitals.

KNIGHTS OF THE TEMPLE

The other major order of the Crusades also started in Jerusalem. In 1119, seven French knights there formed the Knights of the Temple to protect pilgrims. They agreed to live as monks did. Their first home was near what is called the Temple Mount, so they were often called Templars.

Like the Hospitallers, the Templars owned several castles. Noble families in Europe sent their sons to join them, and the wealthy gave donations. Knights from both orders also fought during the Crusades. Muslim generals were said to fear their fighting skill.

So little time, so many castles to run!

85

SPOTLIGHT: SACRED SITES

Need proof of the importance religion played during the Middle Ages? Set your sights on these sites, some of the most magnificent holy places of the era.

DOME OF THE ROCK

Muslim architects were at home with domes, too. The Dome of the Rock was built in Jerusalem during the 690s over a rock at the Temple Mount. Muhammad was said to have been standing on the rock when he was taken to visit heaven. In the Jewish faith, the site is said to be where Abraham prepared to sacrifice his son to God. Inside the building, visitors today can see this famous rock. During part of the Crusades, the Dome of the Rock was used as a Christian church.

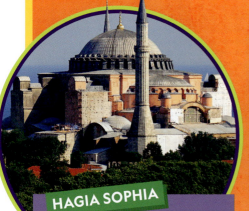

HAGIA SOPHIA

This Byzantine beauty is Hagia Sophia—Greek for "Holy Wisdom." It opened in 537 after Emperor Justinian I built it on the site of an earlier church. Located in his capital of Constantinople, the church was the largest building in the empire, with a main dome that is 160 feet (49 m) high and 105 (32 m) feet across. Some of the marble columns in the church were recycled from older buildings. In 1453, Turkish Muslims took over Constantinople and turned the church into a mosque. It was converted to a museum in the 20th century, before being reclassified as a mosque in 2020.

NOTRE DAME CATHEDRAL

Remember the Goths, one of the tribes that ruined Rome? Their name describes a type of medieval architecture, and Notre Dame is one of the best examples of the Gothic style. Work on the grand church began in Paris in 1163 and went on for almost two centuries. Crusaders prayed here before they set off for the Holy Land. The church is famous for its stained-glass windows and its gargoyles. These small statues of scary creatures were meant to keep evil spirits away.

MAHABODHI TEMPLE

Buddhists believe this spot is where Siddhartha Gautama became enlightened and earned his name of the Buddha. The temple is in Bodh Gaya, in eastern India. The current temple there was built during the fifth or sixth century, replacing an earlier temple built in that spot hundreds of years before. The main tower is 164 feet (50 m) tall, and the entire building is made of brick.

ANGKOR WAT

What, you don't know about Angkor Wat? It's just one of the most famous Hindu temples ever built. The Khmer, a people in what is now Cambodia, built their capital of Angkor around 890. During the 12th century, their king began building Angkor Wat. He saw it as both a temple and a government building. At almost one square mile (2.6 sq km), it's probably the largest religious complex in the world. Carvings on the walls show the most important Hindu gods. Later, rivals of the Khmer took over Angkor and made the temple a Buddhist shrine.

JOKHANG TEMPLE

Tibet developed its own form of Buddhism, and one of its holiest sites is in Lhasa, the country's capital. Jokhang Temple was built during the seventh century, to help spread Buddhist teachings. Monks lived there, and inside were thousands of images of the Buddha and other religious figures. Made of wood and stone, the temple was influenced by building styles from neighboring lands.

87

Inside and Outside NOTRE DAME

Notre Dame wasn't the biggest medieval cathedral, but it's the best known today. It sits on an island in the Seine River, which flows through the heart of Paris. Let's take a look at some of the features found in Notre Dame and other cathedrals.

Spire

The tallest part of most cathedrals is the spire, which is sometimes called a steeple. Notre Dame's original spire was removed because it wasn't stable. Another one was added during the 19th century and is 295 feet (90 m) high.

Bell Tower

Bells were *a-pealin'* during the Middle Ages, and they were often hung and rung in church towers. They rang to note the hours of the day and also to call people to Mass or to mark important occasions. Notre Dame's two bell towers are 226 feet (69 m) high. The South Tower has a bell nicknamed Emmanuel that dates from the 17th century and weighs 14.3 tons (13 t)! The North Tower has nine smaller bells that replaced four put there during the 19th century. Notre Dame's bells were featured in the book and movie *The Hunchback of Notre Dame*. The hunchback hero, Quasimodo, was the church's bell ringer.

A MASSIVE FIRE RAVAGED PARTS OF NOTRE DAME IN 2019. THE FRENCH GOVERNMENT IS REBUILDING IT AND HOPES TO REOPEN IT IN 2024.

INSIDE THE CATHEDRAL

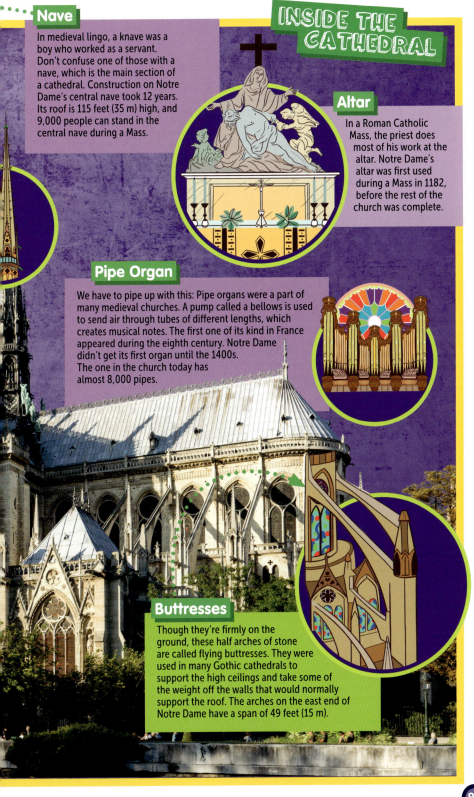

Nave
In medieval lingo, a knave was a boy who worked as a servant. Don't confuse one of those with a nave, which is the main section of a cathedral. Construction on Notre Dame's central nave took 12 years. Its roof is 115 feet (35 m) high, and 9,000 people can stand in the central nave during a Mass.

Altar
In a Roman Catholic Mass, the priest does most of his work at the altar. Notre Dame's altar was first used during a Mass in 1182, before the rest of the church was complete.

Pipe Organ
We have to pipe up with this: Pipe organs were a part of many medieval churches. A pump called a bellows is used to send air through tubes of different lengths, which creates musical notes. The first one of its kind in France appeared during the eighth century. Notre Dame didn't get its first organ until the 1400s. The one in the church today has almost 8,000 pipes.

Buttresses
Though they're firmly on the ground, these half arches of stone are called flying buttresses. They were used in many Gothic cathedrals to support the high ceilings and take some of the weight off the walls that would normally support the roof. The arches on the east end of Notre Dame have a span of 49 feet (15 m).

89

Know Your Medieval Warfare

Armies of the Middle Ages used a variety of tactics and weapons on the battlefield. Now you can learn the score about medieval war.

GREEK FIRE

Greek fire wasn't a kind of medieval hot sauce, but it could make things hot for the enemy. The fire came from a mixture of chemicals that could burn even on water. It was first used by Byzantine sailors during the seventh century. They fired the fiery mix out of tubes, like a flamethrower of sorts. Greek fire was sometimes used in land battles, too.

THE CAVALRY

Warriors had fought on horseback for centuries before the Middle Ages. But in medieval Europe, rulers such as Charlemagne turned to mounted soldiers, or cavalry, more than before. New technology played a part. Stirrups made it easier for soldiers to sit tall in the saddle while swinging a sword or thrusting a lance. Cavalries let generals quickly move some of their troops from one place to another. And while some soldiers fought on horseback, others still hit the ground running, forming what's known as infantry.

COMPOSITE BOWS

In Central Asia, the Mongols and others took aim at enemies using what's called a composite bow. (Composite means it's made from different materials.) A Mongol bow started with a wooden frame, with horn and animal sinew layered on top. Firing while on horseback, a Mongol soldier could launch an arrow 350 yards (320 m)—about the length of three football fields placed end to end! The archers had arrows for all sorts of needs. Some could pierce armor, and some even had tiny grenades on their tip!

90

CROSSBOWS

You didn't want to cross an archer with a crossbow. It packed a wallop that allowed even small archers to become deadly foes, since it was much easier to use than a longbow. Its arrows were also heavier and could sail some 1,000 feet (305 m). In Europe, crossbows became common in combat during the 11th century. They were so deadly, some Christian religious leaders said they shouldn't be used against Christian soldiers. Instead, they said, armies should save them to target nonbelievers.

SIEGE WEAPONS

Medieval armies might *siege* the day—and night, too. During a siege, an army surrounded a city or castle and tried to force the enemy to surrender by cutting off their supplies of food and water. If that didn't work, the besieging army began to fire at the enemy. Before cannons became common, siege weapons included devices such as catapults and trebuchets. Armies could fling stones that weighed up to 1,000 pounds (454 kg) over the enemy's walls. When it came time to storm a castle, the attackers often wheeled up a siege tower. From the tower, soldiers could climb onto the enemy's walls or fire arrows down into the castle or city.

CANNONS

The Chinese perfected gunpowder and the first cannons (see pages 72–73). By the end of the Middle Ages, cannons were making a bang in other countries, too. They were first used in Europe during the 14th century. As the technology for making cannons improved, armies could fire balls that weighed up to 800 pounds (363 kg). In 1453, the Ottoman Turks attacked Constantinople with a mammoth cannon that could fire a ball that weighed more than 1,300 pounds (590 kg)—more than the weight of 900 basketballs!

LONG BOWS

Here's the long and short of it: Longbows were more powerful than short ones. And yew might not know this, but medieval archers made these longbows out of wood from the yew tree. The wood was naturally springy and curved well when the archer pulled back the bow string. A longbow was about six feet (1.8 m) long, and a skilled archer could launch six arrows in one minute. These arrows could travel 600 feet (183 m) or more and could pierce the enemy's armor.

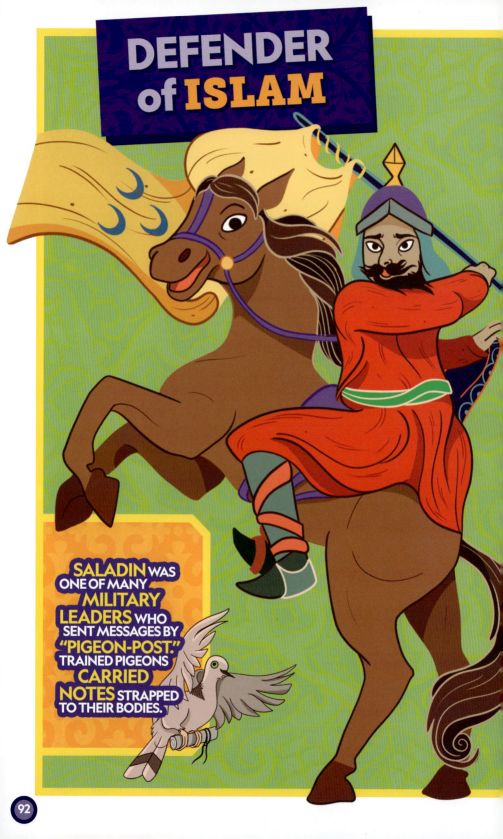

AGE OF THE CRUSADES C. 1137 - 1193 SALADIN

As the Crusades went on, the Christian fighters met their match in the founder of a new Islamic dynasty. His name was Salah al-Din Yusuf ibn Ayyub, but we know him today as Saladin. He was born c. 1137 in what is now Iraq. By the time Saladin was a teen, Islamic fighters had taken back the city of Edessa from the Crusaders. But Muslims in the Holy Land wanted all their land back, and Saladin would deliver the biggest prize.

THE RISE OF SULTAN SALADIN

Saladin's father and uncle served a Muslim leader based in northern Syria. They helped the leader expand his kingdom. When he was still a teenager, Saladin fought for the Syrian ruler, too. At 32, he became commander of the Syrian army, and he had his first taste of the Crusades in 1174. His arrival in Alexandria, Egypt, was enough to scare off Christians attacking the city. That same year, with the death of the Syrian leader he once served, Saladin began to take control of different Syrian cities. He eventually earned the title of sultan, or king.

FIGHTING THE LION

In 1187, Saladin set out to take back those parts of the Holy Land in Frankish hands. After winning several quick victories, he won control of Jerusalem itself. After the residents surrendered, they might have feared a brutal massacre. After all, the Christians had killed thousands of Muslims when they took control. But Saladin let the Christians pay a fee and leave the city.

News of Saladin's victory stirred Europeans to launch the Third Crusade. Leading the charge was Richard the Lionheart of England (see pages 82–83), whose army reached the Holy Land in 1191. Richard scored several victories on his way to Jerusalem. But there, in 1192, Saladin and his troops were waiting, and an outnumbered Richard decided to retreat. Saladin had saved the city from the invaders, but he did let Christians make pilgrimages to the city. The sultan died just one year later. His Ayyubid dynasty ruled over Syria and parts of Egypt and Iraq until the middle of the 13th century.

A GENEROUS GENERAL

In battle, Saladin rode tall in the saddle as he personally led his troops. He fought furiously, and at times he executed enemy prisoners. But Saladin was known to show mercy, as he did with the Christians of Jerusalem. And he seemed to respect his foe, King Richard I. When Saladin heard Richard was sick, he agreed to an English request that he send Richard fruit and snow to help him. The snow came from mountains in lands Saladin controlled. By some accounts, Saladin also sent his own doctor to help Richard. Another time, he sent Richard a new horse after his was killed in battle.

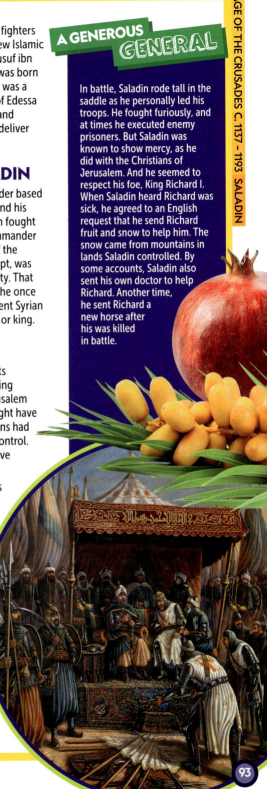

93

ISLAM'S IMPACT

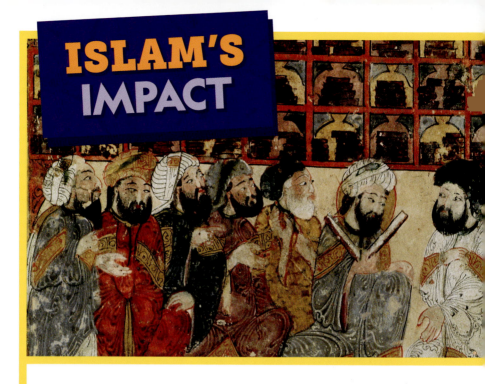

The spread of Islam during the Middle Ages brought a new religion to many parts of the world. It also led to a fantastic explosion of learning. The caliphs of the Muslim world supported these efforts. Ancient texts on science, medicine, and other subjects were available in many of the lands the Arabs conquered. Scholars living in Muslim lands translated these important works into Arabic. They also expanded on the knowledge found in the ancient texts.

Scholars in what had been the western half of the Roman empire did not have access to many of the original ancient texts until the Arabic versions of them were translated into Latin. This began during the 12th century. Through the Arabic works and through trade, new ideas and inventions reached western Europe. And many of them are still important today.

NEW NUMBERS

When you do a math problem, those numbers trace their roots to the Muslim world. The digits 1 through 9 are called Arabic numerals. Muslim math whizzes of the Middle Ages borrowed this numbering system from India and gave the numerals the shapes they have today. Muslim math experts also gave us the form of mathematics called algebra. It uses unknown numbers, often called *x* and *y*, and equations, to solve mathematical problems.

WHAT'S IN A WORD?

Checkmate

This chess term, meaning one player cannot win, comes from the Persian phrase *shah mat*, which means "the king is defeated."

I yield!

MOVING MEDICINE FORWARD

When patients today go "under the knife" for surgery, their doctors are most likely using tools described in Muslim medical books from the Middle Ages. Doctors in Islamic lands used special knives called scalpels to cut open a patient. They also used delicate tools called forceps to hold on to skin.

Muslim countries also introduced the first real hospitals—places where patients received care for many different medical conditions. One of the first was built in Cairo, Egypt, during the ninth century. It treated patients for free. Later hospitals also had schools to train new doctors.

DOWN ON THE FARM

With their wide trade network, Muslims brought new foods from India and China to other parts of Asia and beyond. Some of these crops included oranges, sugar cane, and rice. And it was Muslims who helped spread coffee as a popular drink, first in Asia and Africa. Europeans didn't get their first taste of "joe" until the 17th century.

SKILL WITH MILLS

During the Middle Ages, water was often used to power mills, where grain was turned into flour. But where water was in short supply, Persian inventors came up with the first windmills. Later, windmills were also used to pump water from underground. Most likely, the Crusaders saw windmills on their trips to the Holy Land and brought the invention back to Europe.

FUN AND GAMES

Muslims in the Middle Ages weren't just about growing crops and juggling numbers. They needed their downtime, too. Some of them relaxed by playing chess. The game seems to have been created in India, but when it reached Persia, it became more like the game we play today. Arabs then took the Persian version and spread it across western Asia and Europe.

Playing and listening to music was a favorite pastime. Muslim musicians plucked a stringed instrument called the oud that in Europe developed into the lute. These stringed instruments led to the development of the guitar.

95

SPOTLIGHT: GREAT MUSLIM THINKERS

Who were some of the great scientists and scholars who helped make the Islamic world a great center of learning? Here's a look at several.

WHERE WISDOM LIVED

If you wanted to wise up in medieval Muslim times, you headed to Baghdad, the capital of modern Iraq. In this city was the House of Wisdom, one of the great centers of learning in the Muslim world. It opened in the early ninth century and included a library, an observatory for astronomers, and many rooms for scholars. Al-Kindi and al-Khwarizmi were just two of the great minds who worked there, and many ancient texts were translated in the house.

ONE CALIPH IS SAID TO HAVE PAID SCHOLARS AT THE HOUSE OF WISDOM THE WEIGHT OF EACH BOOK THEY WROTE OR TRANSLATED IN GOLD!

OMAR KHAYYAM

Today, many people know Omar Khayyam as a poet. His *Rubaiyat*, a collection of poems, is still read. But this 11th-century Persian scholar knew his way around numbers, too. He made contributions to algebra, and he sometimes tried to solve algebra problems using methods from geometry. Khayyam also was an astronomer, and he studied the skies to help create a new calendar.

AL-JAZARI

Tick tock, who knew his clocks? A Muslim from Turkey named Ibn al-Razzaz al-Jazari. During the early 13th century, he made a variety of clocks. Some used the movement of water from one bowl to another to mark the passing of time. Al-Jazari was fascinated by mechanical devices of all kinds and wrote a book about them.

AL-KINDI

As scholars in Muslim nations began to translate ancient works on science and philosophy, Abu Yusuf Ya'qub ibn Ishaq al-Kindi helped guide their efforts. Born around 800 in what is now Iraq, he wrote philosophy texts of his own. Al-Kindi thought that one God was the source of all things and that the world would go on forever. In science, he wrote about different medicines and the substances that formed them. He also wrote about music and added a fifth string to an instrument called the oud. In his free time, al-Kindi made a lot of sense about scents—he wrote a book on how to make perfumes.

AVICENNA

The Muslim world knew this doctor and scientist as Ibn Sina, but today he's best known as Avicenna. He was born in what is now Uzbekistan around 970. Abu-'Ali al-Husayn ibn-'Abdallah Ibn-Sina wrote 276 books, though more than 200 of them are no longer available. In his medical writings, Avicenna addressed such things as broken bones and how to fix them, how to make certain medicines, and many different diseases. Doctors followed his advice for centuries, and his writings were translated into Latin and read in Europe.

AL-KHWARIZMI

Whether he was looking down at numbers or up at the stars, Muhammad ibn Musa al-Khwarizmi made an impact on science and math. This great ninth-century Persian scholar helped get algebra off the ground, and he's sometimes called the "father" of this branch of math. Al-Khwarizmi also set down tables of numbers used in trigonometry, another mathematical system. His books, when translated into Latin, helped bring algebra and Arabic numerals to the West. The word "algebra" comes from an Arabic word in one of his book's titles. In addition, with his study of the night sky, al-Khwarizmi helped detail the position of the sun and the planets.

IBN RUSHD

Ibn Rushd was a 12th-century philosopher based in Toledo, Spain. He wrote about the works of one of the great Greek philosophers, Aristotle. During the 1200s, his books on Aristotle were translated into Latin, and many European scholars read the great Greek's ideas for the first time.

97

KING JOHN SIGNS THE MAGNA CARTA.

BARONS Versus A KING

When the great Crusader Richard the Lionheart died in 1199, his brother John became the next king of England—and soon learned that it's not always good to be king. John upset just about everyone he dealt with in one way or another. This included the French, the Roman Catholic pope, and a group of nobles in England called barons. By 1215, the barons weren't bearing it anymore.

AX THE TAX

John's problems started soon after he took the throne. His troubles with France led to him losing territory there that England had controlled. When John decided he wanted to fight to take back the land, he had to raise taxes to do it. So he went to the barons and told them to pay up. The barons' grumbling about the taxes grew in 1214, after the French defeated John's army in a major battle. The barons banded together and said they'd had enough. They began writing the Magna Carta—Latin for "great charter."

98

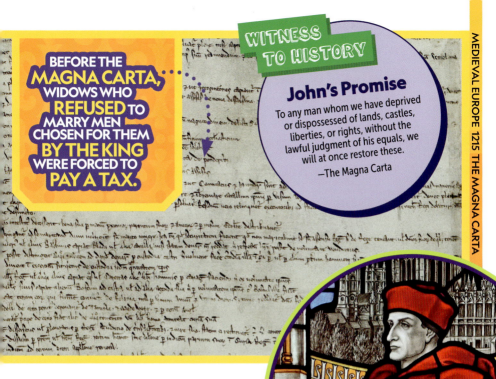

BEFORE THE **MAGNA CARTA**, WIDOWS WHO **REFUSED** TO MARRY MEN CHOSEN FOR THEM **BY THE KING** WERE FORCED TO **PAY A TAX.**

WITNESS TO HISTORY

John's Promise

To any man whom we have deprived or dispossessed of lands, castles, liberties, or rights, without the lawful judgment of his equals, we will at once restore these.

—The Magna Carta

KINGLY DUTIES

The Magna Carta was like a contract between the barons and John. The nobles wanted the king to admit that he couldn't just do anything he wanted. While the barons were vassals and owed John service, they said the king had the duty to treat the barons fairly. And one of his duties was to lay off any new taxes, unless the barons and church leaders approved them. At first, John refused to sign the Magna Carta. But when the rebel barons seized London, the king saw things differently. In 1215, at a spot called Runnymede, John signed the charter.

PROTECTING RIGHTS

The document John signed was not the final version of the Magna Carta. Over the next 10 years, the barons and the next king, Henry III, made changes to it. Today, just three parts of the charter are still part of English law. The one that's had the most impact around the world protected the rights of free men, saying they could not be arrested or jailed without a good reason. This idea led the way to the principle of giving people a free and fair trial if they were accused of a crime—a notion later included in the Constitution of the United States. The Magna Carta also meant that the king or queen was not above the law—though some future English rulers tried their best to test its limits.

A BISHOP WITH THE BARONS

When the barons came to King John with their complaints, Archbishop Stephen Langton was with them. He was the most powerful bishop in England—and not John's first choice for the job. John's refusal to accept Langton led to some of the king's troubles with the pope. Langton was installed as archbishop in 1213, the same year the bishop began to meet with the barons to discuss their issues with the king. He sided with the barons, but he didn't want them to fight the king. He helped write the Magna Carta and played a part in getting John to sign it.

MEDIEVAL EUROPE 1215 THE MAGNA CARTA

99

Tournament TIME

THAT'S ENTERTAINMENT

What started out as a form of military training became a thrilling sport that entertained Europe's nobles and peasants alike. Some tournaments featured parades, and people could buy snacks. Dancers sometimes performed between jousts—like a medieval halftime show. Tournaments were held to mark special events, such as royal weddings, and they could go on for several days. Ladies who had a favorite knight might give him a handkerchief or other small piece of cloth. He would then tie it to his lance. And some knights pretended to be King Arthur or knights of his Round Table.

How did knights sharpen their skills in between battles? They put on their armor, saddled up their horses, and took part in tournaments. Some of these events drew fans who watched knights fight in mock combat. But tournaments were far from being all fun and games.

Well, that escalated quickly.

MEDIEVAL EUROPE JOUSTING

WAYLAID IN A MELEE

These tournaments probably started in France during the 10th century and then spread to other parts of Europe. In the early events, knights took part in what were called melees. Two groups of soldiers battled each other using whatever weapons they could get their hands on. The idea was to kidnap, not kill, the opponents. The knights could take a time-out in an area called a refuge, but otherwise these melees were wild affairs, and some knights ended up dead. But if they stayed alive and won, knights could collect a cash prize. Church and government officials tried to stop these events, but the knights kept on fighting.

COMING TO A POINT

By the 13th century, more tournaments featured a different kind of event: the joust. Tell a knight to knock it off, and he was quick to say yes—if by "it" you meant another knight off his horse. The joust was a duel between two knights on horseback. Each armed with a lance, they rode toward each other on a special field called a list. The goal was to use your lance to send the other knight flying off his mount. The winner of a joust could keep his opponent's horse and armor and sell it back to the loser for a pretty penny.

Jousts had strict rules to try to keep knights from injury and death. The lances did not have sharp ends, and knights wore heavier, thicker armor than what they would usually wear in combat. Most knights looked up just before they made contact with their foe. This kept wooden splinters from a broken lance from blinding them. But it also meant the knight couldn't see what he was doing at that moment! Knights still got hurt, of course, if they fell off their horses or took a particularly hard hit. And some still died, despite trying to play it safe.

DURING ONE JOUST IN THE 15TH CENTURY, A KNIGHT'S HELMET WAS KNOCKED OFF AND FLEW 24 FEET (7.3 M).

101

A KHAN-FIDENT RULER

I totally rule.

While English barons and their kings were squabbling, a great new empire was on the rise. For centuries in Central Asia, different nomadic tribes had raised cattle and sheep on the region's vast grasslands. One tribe, known as the Mongols, sometimes battled their neighbors. As the 13th century began, one Mongol chief emerged as the Genghis Khan, or "Universal Ruler." He created an army that was feared across Asia and into Europe. But Genghis and his sons who ruled after him were more than warriors. They also supported trade and the arts across their lands.

BUILDING AN EMPIRE

Genghis was born with the name Temujin, and was the son of a Mongol chief. Legends say that after his father was killed, Temujin and his family survived by eating whatever they could find—including rodents and badgers. As a young man, Temujin united different Mongol clans under his rule and then defeated enemy tribes.

As Genghis Khan, he ordered that Mongol boys learn how to fight from an early age. His troops were skilled riders and could expertly fire arrows as they rode. On the battlefield, soldiers formed groups of up to 10,000 men. They signaled each other using flags and fires.

Genghis and his army became famous for their harsh tactics, particularly as they invaded Persia in 1219. They massacred whole cities and left behind piles of their enemies' skulls. Persia was just one of many great kingdoms of the day that felt the wrath of the Khan. The Mongols under Genghis took over parts of China and conquered lands as far west as modern Ukraine. They added to their skills on the battlefield by learning how to make siege weapons from the Chinese.

LAW OF THE LAND

While his enemies saw him as a ruthless killer, Genghis wanted order within Mongol society. He drew on some existing customs to set down a code of law called the Great Yasa. This code touched on many parts of life—from how to kill an animal for food to how to punish certain criminals. Someone caught polluting water was executed. So were thieves, spies, and people who refused to share food with strangers. The Yasa also spelled out who was and wasn't taxed. Lawyers, doctors, and religious leaders were among the people who didn't have to pay taxes.

TO MAKE THEIR ARROWS EVEN MORE PAINFUL TO THEIR ENEMIES, THE MONGOLS SOMETIMES DIPPED THE TIPS IN SALT. TO MAKE THE ARROWS DEADLIER, THEY ALSO DIPPED SOME IN POISON.

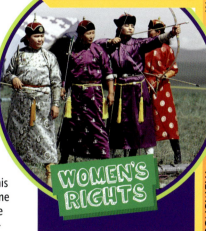

WOMEN'S RIGHTS

Across the medieval world, most women got a raw deal. They usually lacked legal rights and were treated like men's property. Mongol women, though, had it a little better off under Genghis Khan. They had more freedom when choosing who to marry—or whether to get married at all. They also could buy, sell, or trade family property without checking in with a male relative first. That was not true in many countries at that time. Women could also play important roles in society, as shamans or government advisers. Some also learned to ride and shoot, and they fought in the Mongol army. The status of Mongol women sometimes surprised the people Genghis defeated. In their own societies, women were not given these rights.

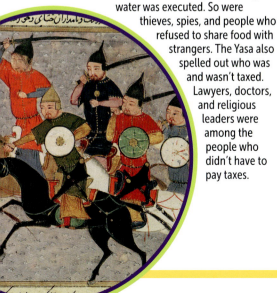

103

ONE Becomes FOUR

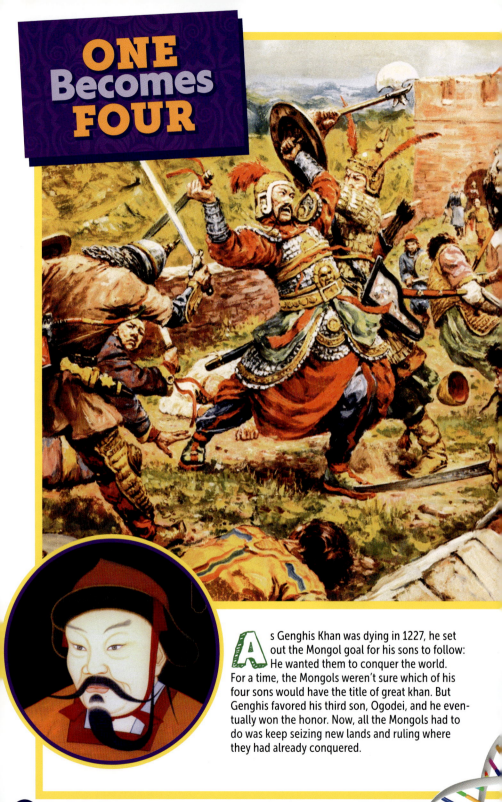

As Genghis Khan was dying in 1227, he set out the Mongol goal for his sons to follow: He wanted them to conquer the world. For a time, the Mongols weren't sure which of his four sons would have the title of great khan. But Genghis favored his third son, Ogodei, and he eventually won the honor. Now, all the Mongols had to do was keep seizing new lands and ruling where they had already conquered.

CREATING THE KHANATES

Ogodei soon divided up his father's empire into four regions, with three of Genghis's surviving sons and one grandson ruling each. The new mini-empires that developed were called khanates. In theory, the great khan ruled over all the lands. But each khanate became an independent state. Over time, the four rulers of the khanates and their sons expanded their realms. One was based in the Mongol homeland of Central Asia. One was in Russia, where the Mongols were called the Golden Horde. Another khanate was based in the former empire of Persia. And the last was in China.

BACK TO THE BATTLEFIELD

Ogodei looked both to the east and the west for new lands. He sent troops farther into China, while other troops attacked Russia. Batu, one of Genghis's grandsons, led the charge through the major Russian cities of Moscow and Kiev. He then headed into Poland and was hungry to take Hungary. The Mongol advance left some Europeans shaking with fear. But then they had some good luck—though it was bad luck for Ogodei. The great khan died in 1241, and Batu soon ended his invasion and returned to the Mongol capital of Karakorum.

Europe was saved, but other places weren't so lucky. In 1258, Mongol troops captured Baghdad, the capital of the Islamic Abbasid dynasty. Their conquests ended though when they were defeated in the Holy Land by an army from Egypt. But Mongols still controlled what was soon called the Ilkhanate.

In China, the Mongols took on the forces of the great Song dynasty. The Song knew a thing or two about warfare (see pages 70–71). And at one point, they amassed an army of more than one million men. Still, after years of battle, the Mongols were able to defeat the Song. Leading them in this Chinese conquest was another grandson of Genghis—Kublai Khan.

A LAND OF MANY FAITHS

The Mongols believed in one supreme god who created everything. Yet they also believed lesser gods existed. And they believed in animism and the power of shamans to keep tabs on the spirit world. As Genghis Khan spread Mongol rule, he didn't force his beliefs on others. The Great Yasa made clear that his people could worship however they chose. Across the khanates, Christianity, Buddhism, Islam, and other religions were followed. Over time, though, some Mongol rulers embraced other faiths. In the Ilkhanate, the ruling family became Muslims.

SCIENTISTS THINK THAT ABOUT 39 MILLION PEOPLE ALIVE TODAY MIGHT BE ABLE TO TRACE THEIR FAMILY ROOTS BACK TO GENGHIS KHAN.

GREATEST of the GREAT

WHAT'S IN A WORD?

Kamikaze

Twice, Kublai Khan tried to attack Japan by sea. And twice his ships were destroyed by powerful storms. The Japanese called such a storm *kamikaze*, meaning "divine wind." During World War II, Japanese pilots who flew suicide missions were called kamikazes.

MEDIEVAL ASIA 13TH CENTURY – 14TH CENTURY KUBLAI KHAN

Of all the great khans who followed Genghis, Kublai Khan is the most famous today. He took the title in 1260, at the age of 45. He had been fighting the Song in China, and as great khan, he was determined to add that empire to his own. Even while still fighting the Song, he declared himself the new emperor of China. He finally could claim complete control of Song lands in 1279, marking the start of his Yuan dynasty.

THE UPS AND DOWNS OF AN EMPEROR

Kublai Khan built a new capital city, Khanbaliq. Today, it's the site of Beijing, the capital of China. He lived in a splendid palace and welcomed visitors from across Asia and Europe. The great khan supported the arts and continued his grandfather's acceptance of all religions in his realm. He also built roads and expanded China's trade with other lands. But Kublai Khan was never close to his Chinese subjects, and they weren't too fond of him or the other Mongols, either.

And despite the warlike ways of the Mongols, Kublai Khan couldn't keep up his military victories. His troops were defeated on land and on sea as they tried to take Japan, Burma, Thailand, and other parts of East Asia. And Mongol horses didn't know what to think when they faced enemy elephants in Burma. The petrified ponies turned and ran!

A SHORT RUN

Kublai Khan died in 1294, and the Mongols who followed him as emperor faced tough times. Plague hit the country and later spread to Europe (see pages 124–127). The cost of some goods soared, and peasants sometimes rebelled. Kublai Khan's Yuan dynasty crashed in 1368, and the Mongols left China.

MARCO'S MARK ON HISTORY

Marco Polo was just a teenager when he started a grand adventure. Traveling with his father and uncle, in 1275 he reached the court of Kublai Khan. There, he served the great khan for 17 years, traveling across China and neighboring lands. When he returned to Italy, Marco Polo wrote about what he had seen and done. *The Travels of Marco Polo* gave Europeans their first detailed look at life in Yuan dynasty China. And his book is still read today.

WITNESS TO HISTORY

Kind Words for the Khan

"Not only was [Kublai Khan] brave and daring in action, but in point of judgment and military skill he was considered to be the most able and successful commander that ever led the [Mongols] to battle."

—*The Travels of Marco Polo*

107

SPOTLIGHT: A LOOK AT BOOKS

Marco Polo was just one medieval writer whose words are still read today. Talented people put quill to paper and told stories to entertain or record history. Here's a look at just a few of the most important books of the Middle Ages.

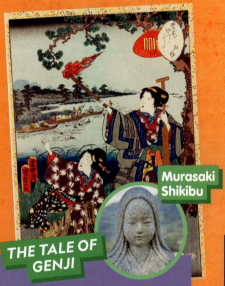

Murasaki Shikibu

THE TALE OF GENJI

Before the rise of shoguns and samurai, Murasaki Shikibu served Empress Shoshi of Japan. She came from a well-educated family, and at the beginning of the 11th century, she wrote *The Tale of Genji*. And what a tale it was. The book is considered one of the world's first novels, and Murasaki used her position at court to share a glimpse of what life was like there. Genji, the main character, is based on one or two real-life emperors. Shikibu showed her readers how Japan's ruling class dated and married in medieval times.

Abu'l Qasim Firdausi

THE SHAHNAMA

Around the same time Murasaki was writing away, Abu'l Qasim Firdausi was finishing up a poem called *The Shahnama*. It is one very long poem—it has 50,000 pairs of rhyming couplets that took Firdausi more than 20 years to write! The poem examines Persian history through the lives of its former rulers. Firdausi mixed in a bit of folklore with his history, and later editions of *The Shahnama* were illustrated with beautiful paintings.

THE DOMESDAY BOOK

No, this is not a guide on how to prepare for domesday. (Domesday is the medieval spelling of doomsday.) The Domesday Book helped William the Conqueror keep control of his new English lands. The name refers to the book God supposedly has with the names of people who will make it into heaven—or not—on doomsday, the last day on Earth. When William's army from Normandy, France, defeated the English in 1066, he became king. And in 1085, he ordered a record of all the land and property owners in his new realm. The Domesday Book also listed the people who worked the land for lords and if the land had valuable resources. All that info helped William figure out how much tax he was owed. The book was the first record of its kind in Europe, and historians later used it to better understand medieval life in England.

THE DIVINE COMEDY

Dante Alighieri

Don't let the title fool you—there's not much to laugh about in this medieval classic. The Italian poet Dante Alighieri began writing *The Divine Comedy* around 1307. In it, the poem's hero travels through heaven, hell, and a place called purgatory. Along the way, the hero—perhaps Dante himself—meets figures from history. He also meets a woman named Beatrice. In real life, Dante loved a woman of the same name, but they didn't have a close relationship. *The Divine Comedy* was considered a masterpiece not long after Dante died in 1321, and it remains one today.

THE ICELANDIC SAGAS

Like anyone else, the Vikings liked to tell one another tales. Some were based on history, while others talked about dwarfs and dragons. Around the start of the 11th century, people began to write down these stories, creating what are called sagas. One saga describes the voyage of Leif Eriksson to a place the Icelanders called Vinland. This is no tall tale—Vinland was Newfoundland, Canada, and Leif and his crew were the first Europeans to set foot in North America. They reached the continent around the year 1000.

DECAMERON

Giovanni Boccaccio

Dante's work influenced another great Italian writer of the Middle Ages: Giovanni Boccaccio. His greatest work was *Decameron*. Boccaccio started it around 1349, as the Black Death (see pages 124–127) was spreading across Europe. In the book, 10 people flee the city of Florence to escape the plague. As they travel, they tell each other stories, which form the heart of the book. Some are funny, some are sad, and some are based on folktales known at the time. Some modern scholars think Boccaccio was offering advice on how to survive the plague.

Second to NUN

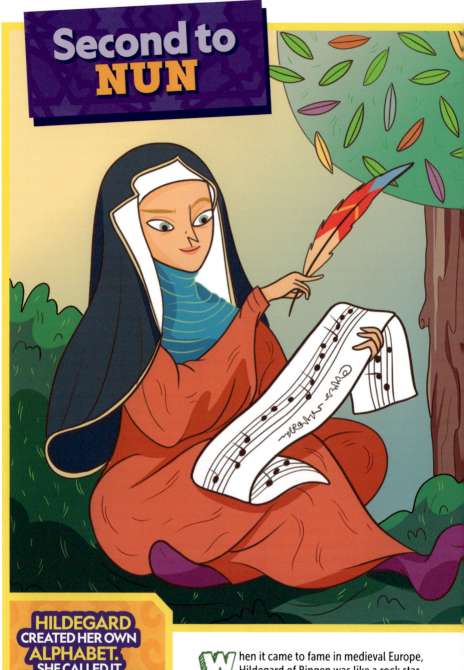

HILDEGARD CREATED HER OWN ALPHABET. SHE CALLED IT *LINGUA IGNOTA*, LATIN FOR "THE UNKNOWN LANGUAGE."

When it came to fame in medieval Europe, Hildegard of Bingen was like a rock star ... if nuns can be rock stars, that is. Hildegard was born in 1098 in Bingen, Germany. She became a nun as a teenager, and like few other women of the Middle Ages, made a big impact with her writings on many subjects.

THE WORD FROM GOD

At a young age, Hildegard was sent to a convent (see sidebar) to live and be educated. She said she could hear and see things others couldn't, and she believed they were messages from God. Hildegard didn't tell others about these visions until later in life. By then, she was the prioress, or head, of a convent. Hildegard thought that God wanted her to share her visions with the world. With the help of a monk, she wrote *Know the Ways* to explain what she thought the visions meant. Hildegard believed that God had both a male and female side—something most men in the church didn't accept. Yet the church did not try to stop her from sharing her ideas, and even the pope liked her book. Other religious and political leaders wrote her, seeking her thoughts on a range of subjects. And she even went on tour, speaking on religious subjects, mostly to men. A woman speaking in public like that was almost unheard of in the Middle Ages.

BUSY

Hildegard didn't stop her writings with *Know the Ways*. She wrote two more books about her visions, plus a play and some poems. She also turned to science. She was skilled at healing the sick, and she wrote two medical books. In one, she describes herbs and other medical treatments, and doctors referred to her works for several centuries. Some of Hildegard's health tips are still championed today: Eat a good diet, get a good night's sleep, and don't get too stressed.

Music was an important part of religious ceremonies, and Hildegard had her hand in that, too. She wrote dozens of hymns—both the words and music—and her tunes are still played and recorded today. She was honored by Roman Catholics for centuries, and in 2012 the church bestowed upon Hildegard its highest honor when it named her a saint.

CONVENT LIFE

Medieval monks in Europe lived in monasteries. For nuns, their home was a convent, also called a nunnery. Many nuns, like Hildegard, came from wealthy families who donated to the convents that educated their daughters. The girls learned to read and write and such skills as weaving and painting. Some women then chose to remain in the convents and become nuns, perhaps because they were deeply religious. In the convent, they could serve God and also care for the poor and sick. Others did not want to get married. Of these, some, like Hildegard, became great scholars.

SCHOOL'S IN

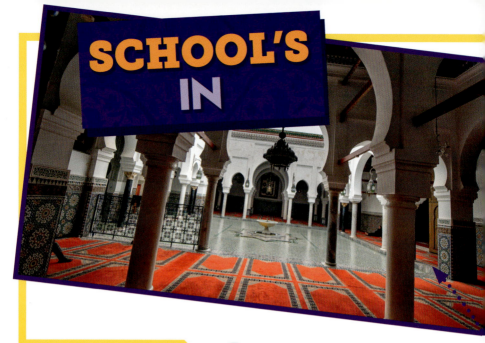

THE **FOUNDER** OF **AL QARAWIYYIN** WAS **FATIMA AL-FIHRI**. SHE USED MONEY SHE **INHERITED** FROM HER WEALTHY FATHER TO START THE **MOSQUE** THAT LATER EXPANDED INTO **A LIBRARY** AND **UNIVERSITY** IN FEZ.

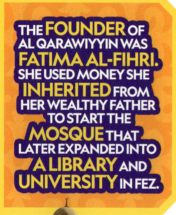

To be more than a farmer or soldier, young people during the Middle Ages needed a good education. In Christian Europe, convents and monasteries were early centers of learning, but they were gradually replaced by universities. These schools were separate from church organizations. In Muslim and Buddhist lands, the first universities were connected to religious sites, such as mosques and temples. Without fail, universities featured the best teachers of the day and produced great scholars.

FEZ WAS FIRST

Al Qarawiyyin is considered the world's oldest existing university. It opened in Fez, Morocco, as a mosque in 859. Scholars there were known for their study of the stars. Another Islamic university opened in Cairo, Egypt, around 971, and it welcomed students from many lands. There soon was one in Timbuktu, Mali, as well, where the best students spent 10 years focusing on one particular topic. The subjects there included geography, history, chemistry, and art; some students also took classes in practical subjects, such as farming and fishing. By the 12th century, the school in Timbuktu had as many students as some large universities have today! In Asia, the temple at Angkor Wat had a university by the late 12th century.

OXFORD, ENGLAND

ISLAMIC LANDS/MEDIEVAL EUROPE   HIGHER LEARNING

EUROPE'S CLASS ACT

Europe started sprouting universities during the ninth century, when a medical school opened in Salerno, Italy. It's often called the first medical school anywhere, as well as the first European university. Its students studied the inside of the human body by dissecting dead bodies. Dissections had not been done since ancient times, and they provided great detail on how the body worked. Unlike many schools at the time, Salerno educated women as well as men.

The Crusades may have played a role in getting other European universities off the ground. Knights returned from the Holy Land with greater knowledge of Muslim learning and translations of ancient books. After Bologna, Italy, opened its university in 1088, more universities began to open outside Italy. Two of the most famous medieval schools were in Paris and in Oxford, England. Students generally entered university when they were 14 and studied for eight years. Their subjects, which included grammar, math, and astronomy, were based on the education given in ancient Greece and Rome. After receiving their degree, students could spend even more time in school to specialize in such subjects as law or medicine.

STUDENTS IN CHARGE

In Italy, students didn't just go to class—they called the shots. This was especially true at the school in Bologna. Students there started the university and elected other students to keep it running. For a time, the students even graded the teachers! If they thought the professors deserved an F for their teaching, the students could vote not to pay them. City leaders, though, put an end to this.

113

Let's EAT!

FOR A WEDDING FEAST KING HENRY III OF ENGLAND THREW IN 1251, CHEFS PREPARED 7,000 CHICKENS, 70,000 FISH AND EELS, AND ALMOST 70,000 LOAVES OF BREAD.

What was on the table for medieval Europeans? That depended on where you lived and what social rank you held. And the weather sometimes played a role in how much people got to eat as well. Too much or too little rain could wipe out crops, leading to famine.

FOOD FIT FOR A KING

For those on top of the social heap, the daily meals might feature a variety of food. By law, only nobles could hunt in the forests on their lands. This meant that a deer or rabbit from the woods could end up on their plates. Nobles could also afford to raise livestock, such as sheep and cows, for meat.

The menu got even fancier when nobles held a feast. Tables were filled with such dishes as peacock and other birds, and royal chefs presented them in clever ways. A roasted bird might be served with its feathers all around it, or an animal might be stuffed back into its skin. After the Crusades, spices from Asia became more common. Sugar, though, was a rare treat and was sometimes locked up because it was so valuable. Some nobles had their own orchards, so they could serve fruit or nuts for dessert. Diners used their hands as utensils and stale pieces of bread as plates.

PEASANTS

For a lord's peasants, mealtime was a little bit boring. Everyone ate bread in medieval Europe, but farmers used grains such as barley and rye, which the nobles considered less desirable than wheat. Barley also turned up in soups and porridge. It was the key ingredient in ale, a type of beer that was a common drink for peasants. Bread was also made from oats and peas. This low-quality bread was called horse bread because it was sometimes shared with the animals.

Peasants often raised cows and sheep for their milk, which they turned into butter and cheese. (Fridges didn't exist, and these dairy foods lasted longer than milk.) The poor also raised chickens for their eggs. Meat and fish were rare dishes for the lower classes. Fish was a little more common as a main meal, since Roman Catholic teachings call for not eating meat on certain days. Foreign spices were too expensive for these folks, so they grew herbs to add more flavor to their food.

FAMINE IN THE 14TH CENTURY

Starting in 1315, farmers in northern Europe noticed something was different. Heavy spring rains led to massive flooding that kept farmers from planting their usual crops. Then a pattern of cool summers and longer winters set in. These changes led to a major famine in parts of Europe. To survive, some people ate roots and tree bark, and some ate their farm animals. Finally, the heavy rains began to let up, and by around 1322, farmers were once again able to grow enough food for everyone. But by then the Great Famine had killed millions of Europeans.

Who are you calling boring?

HOUSIN' Around

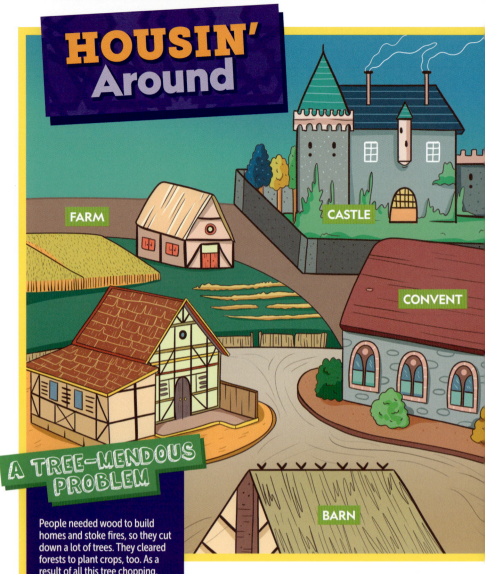

A TREE-MENDOUS PROBLEM

People needed wood to build homes and stoke fires, so they cut down a lot of trees. They cleared forests to plant crops, too. As a result of all this tree chopping, the landscape of Europe changed a lot throughout the Middle Ages. Areas once filled with forests were without any trees. As a result, animals that once lived in the forests lost their homes, reducing the supply of meat that hunters could bring home. Without trees, water could flow onto farms, washing away the soil. By the 13th century, the shortage of wood led some Europeans to burn a new fuel source—coal. But coal soon presented a new set of problems because burning it created air pollution.

Along with food, having shelter is key to staying alive and well. For Europeans in the Middle Ages, homes ranged from palaces and manor houses to simple one-room cottages. (There were castles, too, and you can read about them on pages 138–139.)

MIND YOUR MANORS

A medieval noble's lands were called a manor, and the home he built for himself was called a manor house. The lord of the manor, his family, and his servants all lived there. But the house was more than just a home. At times, it could serve as a little fort, with stone walls

116

MEDIEVAL EUROPE | HOUSING

and a moat to keep out invaders. Wealthier lords built their homes of stone, while others relied mostly on wood. A manor usually had a large room called a hall, where the lord met visitors to discuss business. He and his family ate there, too.

Around the main house were smaller buildings. These included a kitchen and a brewery for making ale. Keeping the kitchen separate lowered the risk of a fire there burning down the main house. The other buildings might also include kennels for a lord's hunting hounds and a barn to store grain.

TINY HOUSES

On the lord's manor, things weren't quite as cushy for the peasants. Their simple homes usually had just one or two rooms. They might be awakened in the night by a moo or an oink, since they often had to share their homes with their farm animals. Some peasant homes were made of solid wood, but many were built out of pieces of twigs twisted together. Then a mud-like muck called daub was used to fill in the cracks. Roofs were usually thatched.

Inside, these simple homes often had dirt or clay floors, with maybe some hay thrown on top. The windows opened to the outside world—they had no glass. A fire in the center of the house provided light, heat, and a place to cook. The peasants slept on straw. And if they needed to go to the bathroom at night, they kept a pot nearby: The bathroom was outside, and making that walk on a cold night was no fun.

117

CLOTHES MINDED

My, you're looking regal.

FROM **ANCIENT TIMES** THROUGH THE MIDDLE AGES, **DARK PURPLE** CLOTHING WAS LINKED TO **ROYALTY** BECAUSE THE DYE USED WAS RARE—IT CAME FROM **TINY, CRUSHED SHELLFISH.**

People wear clothing to keep warm and dry. But clothing also says a lot about someone's position in society—and if they have a flair for fashion. These things were just as true in medieval Europe as they are today.

A FEEL FOR FABRICS

Medieval clothing was made from natural substances. Wool from sheep provided warmth and protected people from the rain. Linen, spun from the flax plant, was good for lightweight clothing or underwear. (Clothes made of linen also were easy to wash, compared with wool, which wasn't.) Some cotton was grown in southern Europe or brought in from other countries, but it was rarely used for clothing because medieval spinners had a hard time turning the puffy balls into thread. The wealthy could dress to impress by wearing items made of silk.

Once thread was spun and woven into fabric, it could be dyed. Dyes came from natural substances, too, and the color options were limited. These natural dyes also faded over time, so clothing soon looked pretty bland. The rich, though, could afford to dye their clothing again. Nobles and wealthy merchants could also show off by adding expensive fur to their clothing.

MEDIEVAL EUROPE CLOTHING

WHO WORE WHAT

Rich and poor alike wore clothes of the same style, though the rich used finer cloths. A typical outfit for men started with braies, which were breeches or trousers that went down to the knees or so. From the feet up to the bottom of the braies the men wore long socks. Next came a long linen shirt, and on top of that was a long piece of clothing called a tunic. Another tunic might go over that when the weather was bad. For a hat, a man might wear a piece of linen cloth that tied under his chin.

Women wore some similar clothing, except for the braies. Their tunics were usually longer, too. And they were expected to keep their arms and legs covered when they were in public. A woman's hat might be simple linen, too, though some women wore wimples, which went under their chin and around their neck. For both men and women, pins and belts helped hold their clothing together. Buttons didn't become common until the 14th century.

Nice threads.

DON'T WEAR THAT—OR ELSE!

In 14th-century London, you had to choose what to wear with care. Special laws made it illegal for people to wear certain items if they were not wealthy. Rich nobles could wear what they wanted, but people below them in status were restricted in what to wear, depending on their income. The laws limited how much the people could spend on certain fabrics or whether they could wear silk, gold, or silver. Women could only wear certain furs, depending on their status.

119

How to Be a MEDIEVAL KID

IN 12TH-CENTURY ENGLAND, BOYS AS YOUNG AS 15 YEARS OLD COULD BE CALLED TO SERVE IN LOCAL ARMED FORCES, CALLED MILITIA.

Being a kid in medieval Europe wasn't always easy. Lots of children got very sick at an early age. And you didn't have much time to enjoy growing up. By the age of 13 or so, kids were considered adults, and some got married at that age. But children during the Middle Ages usually had loving parents and time to play. Here's how your life might have looked if you were a medieval kid.

EARLY YEARS

For your first seven years or so, if you stayed healthy, life was fairly easy as a medieval kid. Pretty much all you did was eat, sleep, and play. After that, you might do small chores around the home. For a girl, this might mean taking care of a younger brother or sister or learning how to cook or turn milk into butter. Young boys did some of the easier farm work, such as keeping birds away from the crops. And all kids were expected to mind their manners, especially if they were ever around nobility. Some books advised children not to pick their nose or burp in public.

Things might be a little different if your family was wealthy. A boy might go to a lord's house to learn how to be a knight. A girl would learn how to run a home and, when she got older, would have servants to do household chores.

HITTING THE BOOKS

During the early centuries of the Middle Ages, most children received little education. It was different, though, if their parents wanted them to be monks or nuns. Then they went to the local monastery or convent to live and learn. During the 11th century in England, public schools appeared. Most of the students were boys, while girls were educated at home. As the Middle Ages went on, more people in cities who were trained as professionals, such as doctors and lawyers, could read and write, but farm kids usually lacked a good education.

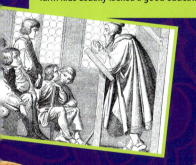

LEARNING THE ROPES

If you were a kid—but more often a boy—who lived in or near a larger community or city, your parents might send you away to learn a trade. You became an apprentice to someone who had a particular skill, such as making knives or working with gold. Apprentices were expected to obey their masters and help in their workshops as they learned the skills that would later lead to a job. Some girls became apprentices, too, learning such skills as baking bread or making certain items out of cloth.

PLAYTIME

For medieval children, there was plenty of play. You would have enjoyed some games and activities similar to those children play today. They included riding a seesaw and playing hide-and-seek and leapfrog. Ball games included early versions of soccer and tennis. As a baby, you probably would have played with a rattle. As you got older, you might get a toy knight if you were a boy and a doll—called a poppet—if you were a girl.

City Life in WESTERN EUROPE

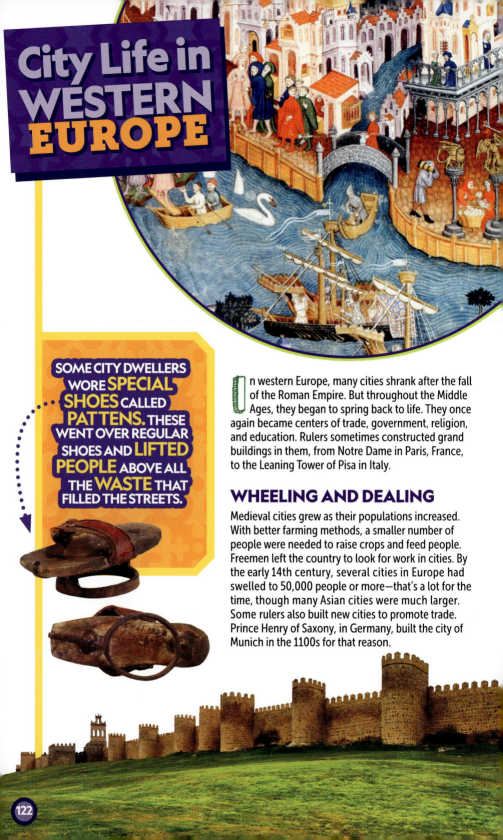

SOME CITY DWELLERS WORE **SPECIAL SHOES** CALLED **PATTENS.** THESE WENT OVER REGULAR SHOES AND **LIFTED PEOPLE** ABOVE ALL THE **WASTE** THAT FILLED THE STREETS.

In western Europe, many cities shrank after the fall of the Roman Empire. But throughout the Middle Ages, they began to spring back to life. They once again became centers of trade, government, religion, and education. Rulers sometimes constructed grand buildings in them, from Notre Dame in Paris, France, to the Leaning Tower of Pisa in Italy.

WHEELING AND DEALING

Medieval cities grew as their populations increased. With better farming methods, a smaller number of people were needed to raise crops and feed people. Freemen left the country to look for work in cities. By the early 14th century, several cities in Europe had swelled to 50,000 people or more—that's a lot for the time, though many Asian cities were much larger. Some rulers also built new cities to promote trade. Prince Henry of Saxony, in Germany, built the city of Munich in the 1100s for that reason.

122

In northern Italy, several major cities rose in power during the 12th century based on trade. They were independent, though they often pledged loyalty to a king. Venice was the most important of these cities, but Florence and Genoa grew powerful, too. In these cities and across Europe, merchants and craftspeople in the same business often set up shop in the same neighborhood.

As centers of wealth and riches, cities were sometimes targets of raiders. To protect cities and towns, the people put up stone walls, and many of these still stand in old European cities.

STINKY STREETS

In cities, death was a threat from many sources. Living jammed together in close quarters, city dwellers could easily catch deadly diseases, such as the Black Death (see pages 124–127). Even though city living might not always kill them, residents did have to put up with some pretty nasty smells: With the wide use of indoor plumbing still hundreds of years away, people often emptied their chamber pots into the streets. And slaughterhouses, which killed livestock for meat, dumped the leftover animal parts next to the human waste. Live farm animals often roamed the streets, going to the bathroom wherever they pleased. This just added to the stench.

A DIRTY JOB ...

But somebody had to do it. That somebody was called a gong farmer, and "it" was getting rid of human waste that didn't end up in the streets. Some towns had large pits called latrines where people went to the bathroom. The waste collected in the pit until the gong farmer came to empty it. ("Gong" was a slang word for human waste.) These "farmers" worked at night and shoveled the waste into a cart. Then they took it outside the city to bury it or spread it on farm fields as a fertilizer.

LOOK OUT BELOW!

When emptying their chamber pots out in the streets, the French tried to be kind. If they let loose from an upstairs window, they called down to the street, "Garde a l'eau!" This meant, "Watch out for water!" Of course, the liquid that fell on a passerby wasn't water. In Scotland, the French expression became "gardy loo."

WITNESS TO HISTORY

Paris Pee-Yew

"The inhabitants of Paris ... forget its evil odor and only notice it when they return from a journey."
—Unknown visitor to Paris, around 1200

The DEADLIEST DISEASE

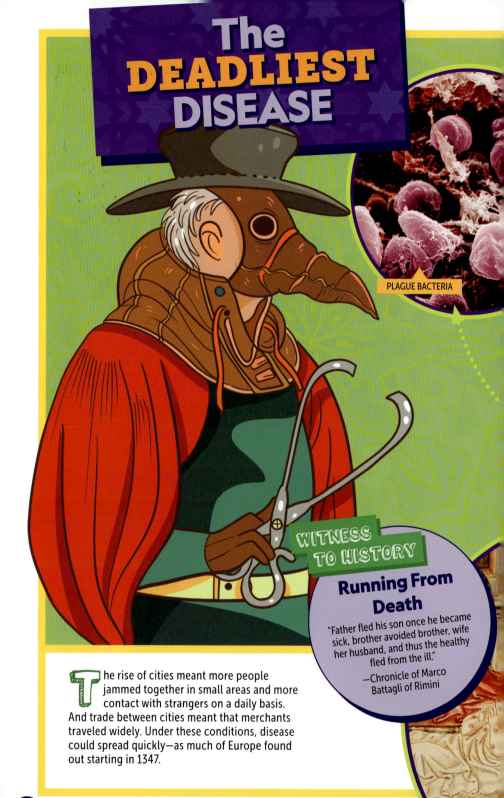

PLAGUE BATERIA

WITNESS TO HISTORY

Running From Death

"Father fled his son once he became sick, brother avoided brother, wife her husband, and thus the healthy fled from the ill."
—Chronicle of Marco Battagli of Rimini

The rise of cities meant more people jammed together in small areas and more contact with strangers on a daily basis. And trade between cities meant that merchants traveled widely. Under these conditions, disease could spread quickly—as much of Europe found out starting in 1347.

BAD BUGS

Sometime during the 14th century, bubonic plague began to spread in Asia. People knew about the plague from the deadly outbreak during the sixth century (see page 23). In 1345, Mongol soldiers brought the disease with them to a region called Crimea. Italian sailors in a port there then brought the plague to Sicily. It continued to spread through Europe and eventually reached North Africa and the Middle East, too. The bacterium that caused the disease lives inside fleas and lice. When these insects bit humans, they spread the plague. It spread even more as sick people coughed or sneezed on the people around them.

We really bugged Europe.

THE BLACK DEATH

Once the plague took hold in Europe, it spread quickly. At the time, it was called the Great Pestilence, and at its worst, the plague killed millions over several years. When someone got the plague, they experienced swelling in their armpits and groin, and then black splotches sprouted on their skin. This earned the plague the name we know it by today: the Black Death. But before dying, victims would suffer horribly, with chills and a fever first, then intense pain. They would throw up over and over, and cough up blood. Within three or four days of catching the plague, they'd likely be dead.

The Black Death struck people of all social ranks, though it was more common in cities. People often caught the disease by inhaling the breath of someone who already had it. This led some people to flee their sick relatives, so they wouldn't get sick, too. Some cities set up guards at their borders, to keep out strangers who might be carrying the disease. And the disease brought out the worst in some people. They falsely accused the Jewish population of causing the plague and carried out hate crimes against them.

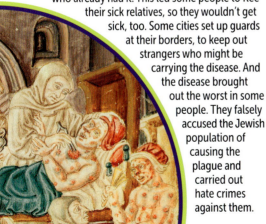

SOME MEDIEVAL DOCTORS TRIED TO CURE THE PLAGUE BY RUBBING THEIR SICK PATIENTS WITH ONION, HERBS, OR EVEN PIECES OF A DEAD SNAKE!

A SHRINKING POPULATION

The Black Death did not hit all parts of Europe in the same way. Florence, Italy, lost about two-thirds of its population, and Paris about half. But some small villages in Germany and England had very few deaths. Because government officials did not always keep good records, it's impossible to know how many people died. The estimates are that about 25 million people in Europe died—up to half the continent's whole population! Another 25 million died in Africa and the Middle East.

MEDIEVAL EUROPE 1347 – 1352 THE BLACK DEATH

125

Dealing With DEATH

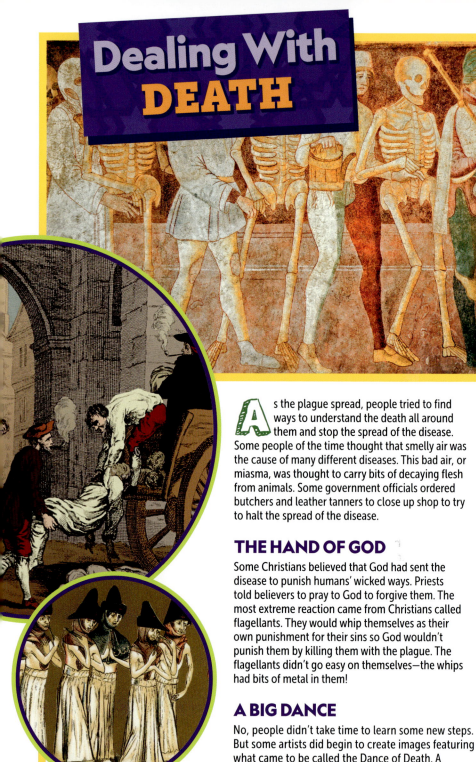

FLAGELLANTS OF TOURNAI

As the plague spread, people tried to find ways to understand the death all around them and stop the spread of the disease. Some people of the time thought that smelly air was the cause of many different diseases. This bad air, or miasma, was thought to carry bits of decaying flesh from animals. Some government officials ordered butchers and leather tanners to close up shop to try to halt the spread of the disease.

THE HAND OF GOD

Some Christians believed that God had sent the disease to punish humans' wicked ways. Priests told believers to pray to God to forgive them. The most extreme reaction came from Christians called flagellants. They would whip themselves as their own punishment for their sins so God wouldn't punish them by killing them with the plague. The flagellants didn't go easy on themselves—the whips had bits of metal in them!

A BIG DANCE

No, people didn't take time to learn some new steps. But some artists did begin to create images featuring what came to be called the Dance of Death. A skeleton represented death, and he was shown

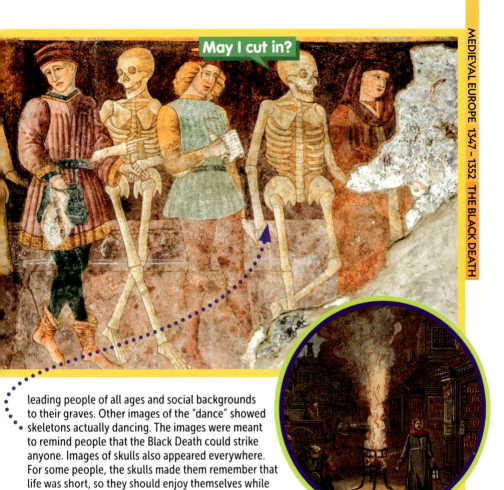

leading people of all ages and social backgrounds to their graves. Other images of the "dance" showed skeletons actually dancing. The images were meant to remind people that the Black Death could strike anyone. Images of skulls also appeared everywhere. For some people, the skulls made them remember that life was short, so they should enjoy themselves while they could.

WAVES OF PLAGUE

The Black Death that began spreading across Europe in 1347 began to lose its punch around 1352. But the plague didn't completely disappear. New waves of the disease broke out several times during the rest of the 14th century. But none of these waves matched the destruction of the Black Death. Plagues hit Europe after the Middle Ages, too. In 1665–66, plague killed about 100,000 people in London.

AFTER THE PLAGUE

The Black Death led officials across Europe to take public health more seriously. Some cities created boards that could limit people's movements when plague struck again. Venice, Italy, set up a special station away from the city where sailors had to stay if there was a chance they might be carrying a disease.

FORTY-DAY STAY

Officials in Venice early on suspected the plague had foreign roots. In 1348, they ordered sailors arriving from abroad to isolate for 40 days. Some other cities copied this. Separating suspected sick people from others is called a quarantine—from the Italian word for "forty." Today, some people are still placed under quarantine if they might possibly spread a serious disease to others.

127

Know Your Home Remedies

There was no cure for the Black Death. But for some illnesses not related to the plague, treatments may have been found in a book of remedies kept by either a trained doctor or a person who practiced folk medicine using knowledge they had learned from relatives. Here are some medieval medical remedies once used in Europe.

A POTENT POTION

A medical mix called St. Paul's potion was said to cure several illnesses, including an upset stomach. The drink contained a variety of herbs and spices, including licorice, fennel, and something called dragon's blood. No, it wasn't really blood—or from a dragon. It was red resin from several different plants. But the recipe for this potion did call for some actual blood, from a bird called a cormorant.

WINE FOR WOUNDS

If you were cut, someone might have called for wine—not to drink but to wash out the wound. Medieval doctors didn't know that bacteria caused infection. But they knew that wine would keep a wound from getting infected: The alcohol in the drink helped kill the bad bacteria.

BUGS TO THE RESCUE

Small stones can sometimes form in certain organs, such as the kidney or bladder. What could help get rid of a bladder stone? Some doctors of the Middle Ages thought insects could do the trick. One medieval healer called for cutting off the heads of dung beetles and crickets and frying them in oil. Then, after letting the bugs sit, he pounded them into a paste and put them on the sick person's body.

MASTERING MIGRAINES

Migraines are a particularly nasty kind of headache that can strike some people out of the blue. What to do? Well, in the Middle Ages, you could have made a concoction with barley and the herbs betony and vervain. These were boiled together, then placed in a cloth and pressed against the head.

SNAIL SLIME

When someone accidentally burned themselves, a small snail could come to the rescue. Burn victims were told to take a live snail and rub its slime on the wound. Modern medicine has shown that medieval docs were on to something: The slime contains chemicals that can reduce pain and prevent infections.

POISON

What to do if a poisonous snake bit you? Reach for a medicine called theriac. The first recipes for this treatment for bites of all kinds went back to Roman times, and over the years, various medical experts added ingredients to the mix. Theriac contained flesh from a viper, a type of snake, and various herbs and minerals added to honey. Its name came from the Greek word *theriakos*, or "wild beast." It was first used for dog, snake, and other animal bites.

129

SPOTLIGHT: WORKIN' FOR A LIVING

Is it lunch break yet?

You know that medieval Europe had a few main social groups (see pages 60–61). Nobles and knights fought, priests prayed and studied, and peasants worked the land. But cities and towns needed people with special skills to keep things humming. Here's a look at just some jobs from the Middle Ages.

GO FOR THE GUILD

Workers who specialized in a craft usually joined a guild. These organizations appeared in cities across Europe. Running the show in the guilds were men with the greatest skill, called masters. They set the rules for who could join a guild and sometimes limited how many hours their members could work. Below the masters were journeymen, who had all the skills of their trade and worked for a master. At the bottom were apprentices, who were just learning their trade (see page 121). It wasn't all work and no play for the guilds. Many built their own halls, where they had parties and other events. Some guilds also built roads and schools.

WOMEN AT WORK

Men dominated the trades in cities, but some women got into the act, too. This was true in Paris during the 13th century. Women often learned their skill from their husbands and kept up his business if he died. Others learned from their fathers, and women could earn the rank of journeymen and help their husbands train apprentices. For most of the Middle Ages in northern Europe, women brewed beer at home for their families. But in some countries, such as Holland and England, women called alewives earned a pretty penny selling it to strangers.

130

IN THE MOOD FOR FOOD

Just like today, people strolling through the markets of medieval cities might work up an appetite. If they were far from home, they could buy a snack or the evening's meal. The people making and selling food in these outdoor markets included butchers, bakers, and piemakers. But not all the food looked good: Bakers in Paris were allowed to sell bread they might have scorched in the oven—or that a rat may have nibbled at.

GOOD SOLES

To give their feet a treat, medieval folks sought out a cordwainer. This was the person who took bits of leather and turned them into new shoes. The leather might have come from goats or sheep killed by the local butcher. In England, there was a distinction between someone who made new shoes and someone who repaired old ones. The repairing job went to cobblers, and from their work we get the phrase "to cobble together," or to make something from different parts.

WHAT'S IN A WORD?

Cordwainer

"Cordwainer" has its roots in the Spanish word *cordovano*, which refers to leather from the city of Cordova (Cordoba), Spain.

YEARNING FOR YARN

Textiles have nothing to do with texting—they're materials used to make cloth. And making textiles was big business in parts of Europe in the last centuries of the Middle Ages. Several cities in what is now Belgium became textile centers, as people turned raw wool into yarn and then wove it into cloth. Spinning and weaving were the work of women on manors, but in cities men took over these jobs. The textile industry also hired fullers to clean the wool and dyers to make it different colors.

FORGING AHEAD

Smiths were people who worked with metal, turning the raw material into something to sell. Goldsmiths made things out of, well, gold, but sometimes silver, too. They produced jewelry, as well as decorations for churches or a noble's home. Some smiths specialized in making just one item, such as buckles made of copper. The hardest-working smiths may have been the blacksmiths. They made everything from suits of armor and swords for knights to a peasant's simple pot. It was hot and dirty work, as the smiths had to heat the metal to very high temperatures before banging it into shape.

131

Nobody's FOOL

A **FRENCH JESTER** NAMED **TRIBOULET** ONCE TOLD ONE BAD JOKE TOO MANY AND WAS **SENTENCED** TO BE **EXECUTED.** HIS KING ASKED HOW HE WANTED TO DIE, AND TRIBOULET SAID, **"OF OLD AGE."** THE KING LET HIM LIVE.

Jest in case you were wondering—you could actually get paid in medieval times for playing the fool. But only a few wealthy nobles and kings hired fools, or jesters, so getting into that business wasn't easy.

THE BEST JESTERS

A jester often had many skills. When his master held a feast, the jester joked, told stories, and sang and danced. Some jesters were also jugglers. With all their skills, jesters were usually well educated, too. No foolin'—jesters could earn decent money. They were paid for performing at weddings and other events.

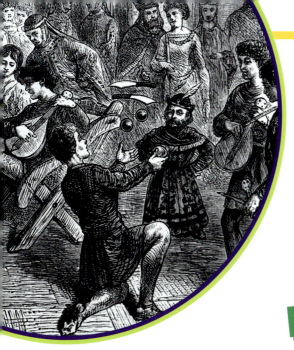

Jest go with it.

FOOLING FOR FUN

Edward II of England paid one jester for expertly playing a trick on him when the king did not expect it. Favored jesters might also get land or horses from a king. One lucky jester named Roland le Pettour received land when he retired. But he was expected to come back to the king's court once a year to entertain. Robert's skills included whistling—and farting!

NOT ALL FUN AND GAMES

But fools did more than fool around. During wartime, jesters went to the battlefield, just like other king's men. Thought to be a fool, a man named Turold is shown on a famous piece of art called the Bayeux Tapestry, which records the conquest of England by William the Conqueror. In it, Turold is seen looking after soldiers' horses. Jesters also sometimes took messages to the enemy's commander.

Jesters might also go to the front lines and show off their juggling skills—using swords! At the same time, they would shout insults to the enemy. The idea was to anger their foes so they would rush into the open to kill the fool and make themselves an easy target. But fools also had less dangerous wartime roles. Before a big battle, they might entertain the troops to boost their spirits.

You might have seen the joker in a deck of cards, dressed in a hat with two or three drooping points and wearing pointy shoes. Many people think of that costume when they think of a medieval jester. But professional fools often dressed like their masters. It was usually fools who entertained for fun who wore the other garb. These fools might belong to amateur groups that were popular in France. They put on their costumes and danced through the streets during festival days.

133

Do the RIGHT THING

WHAT'S IN A WORD?

Chivalry
In French, the word for horse is *cheval*, and knights were called *chevalers*, which is related to the word "chivalry."

Many of the stories of the Middle Ages deal with knights and their heroics on the battlefield. But being a good knight meant more than just swinging a sword. When not riding into a fight, knights were supposed to behave in certain ways. The code that described how a good knight should live was called chivalry.

DEFENDERS OF THE WEAK

For the Roman Catholic Church, asking knights to be chivalrous helped end attacks on peasants. Before the code, some knights robbed rather than defended. With chivalry, knights were supposed to protect the ill, widows, and others who couldn't defend themselves. The code also demanded that knights be loyal, keep their promises, and be good Christians. They shouldn't boast about themselves, and they should be courageous on the battlefield. The values of chivalry influenced many of the knights who joined the orders that fought during the Crusades (see pages 84–85).

A SPECIAL KIND OF LOVE

In songs and stories, chivalrous knights often found themselves in love with a woman. But the woman, alas, was not someone the knight could marry, usually because she was already married. But that didn't keep the knight from loving her or promising to fight bravely in her name. A group of English soldiers once went off to battle in France, each wearing a patch over one eye and promising not to take it off until he had killed an enemy soldier for his beloved. Other knights fought in jousts to try to prove their love.

SINGING'S THE THING

This kind of love between a knight and a lady was called courtly love. People across Europe heard tales of courtly love and chivalrous acts from singers known as troubadours. They were poets and musicians who traveled from one court to another to sing their songs. Troubadours first appeared in southern France during the 12th century, though troubadours performed in many parts of Europe. Noble women seemed especially fond of the troubadour's love songs.

ROLLIN' WITH ROLAND

Not all the poems about chivalrous knights dealt with courtly love. Some long poems, called epics, told of the bravery of knights at war. One of the most famous is *The Song of Roland*, written in northern France during the 11th century. Roland was a real person—he served Charlemagne during the eighth century. But the unknown poet who wrote his "song" changed some of the facts to create a more dramatic story. In the poem, Roland was betrayed in battle, and his enemies were Muslims from Spain. But the poem wasn't supposed to be history: The goal was to hold up chivalry as a path for other knights to follow.

SPOTLIGHT: LEGENDS and LORE

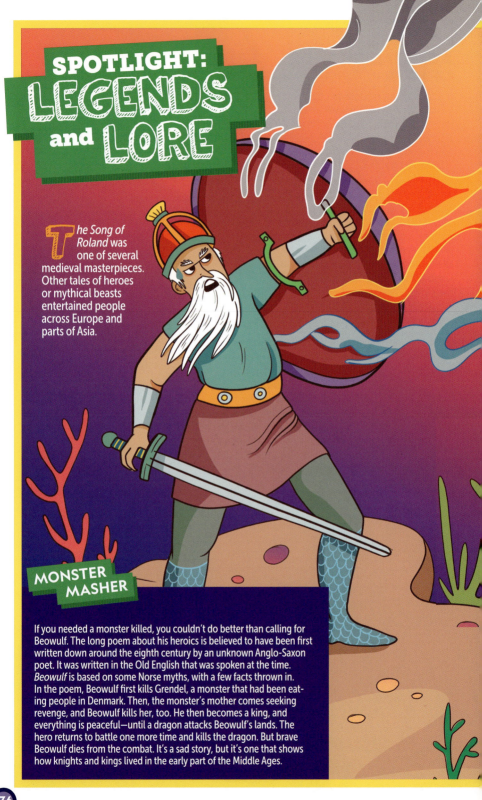

The Song of Roland was one of several medieval masterpieces. Other tales of heroes or mythical beasts entertained people across Europe and parts of Asia.

MONSTER MASHER

If you needed a monster killed, you couldn't do better than calling for Beowulf. The long poem about his heroics is believed to have been first written down around the eighth century by an unknown Anglo-Saxon poet. It was written in the Old English that was spoken at the time. *Beowulf* is based on some Norse myths, with a few facts thrown in. In the poem, Beowulf first kills Grendel, a monster that had been eating people in Denmark. Then, the monster's mother comes seeking revenge, and Beowulf kills her, too. He then becomes a king, and everything is peaceful—until a dragon attacks Beowulf's lands. The hero returns to battle one more time and kills the dragon. But brave Beowulf dies from the combat. It's a sad story, but it's one that shows how knights and kings lived in the early part of the Middle Ages.

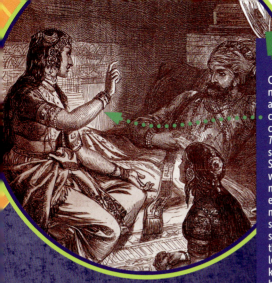

BEDTIME STORIES

Could you tell stories almost every night for three years if it meant staying alive? That's what the fictional character Scheherazade did in the collection of folk tales called *The Thousand and One Nights*. (The story is sometimes called *The Arabian Nights*.) Scheherazade's king was mad at all women, and he killed each new wife he married. Scheherazade had an idea for ending the king's killing ways. She married him, then started telling him a story. Just as her tale was getting good, she stopped, forcing the king to wait till the next night to hear the end. The king loved the stories so much that he didn't kill Scheherazade. The tales she told blended folk stories and myths from India, Persia, and Arab lands. Some of the stories included in *The Thousand and One Nights* were added after the Middle Ages. They include stories well known today, such as Aladdin and his lamp and Sinbad the Sailor.

I'm sword of a big deal.

THE KING OF THE LEGENDS

A magic sword, a wizard, gallant knights, a cool castle—the story of King Arthur has it all. During the Middle Ages, many tales spread about this king, who may have been based on a real king in England ... or, maybe not. No one's sure. But to the people who heard or read about Arthur and his court, the legends are full of excitement. Arthur lived at Camelot and was served by his Knights of the Round Table. His best friend was a knight named Lancelot, and his queen was Guinevere. When Arthur needed some magical mojo, he turned to his wizard Merlin. And on the battlefield, Arthur's sword Excalibur was so bright it could blind his enemies long enough for the king to kill them. Troubadours told some of the tales of Arthur and his world, which were filled with chivalry and courtly love. Several writers also wrote some of the stories down, helping them spread beyond Europe. In modern times, Arthur and other characters from his world sometimes appear in movies.

TELL'S SWELL TALE

Here's the point—William Tell knew how to shoot an arrow. At least, that's what the story about him says. According to the legend, this Swiss archer lived during the 14th century. An Austrian king controlled the land then, and one of his officials in Switzerland wanted Bill to pay his respects to the king. Tell refused, so the official told him to shoot an apple off his son's head or both father and son would be executed. Well, Tell didn't miss, but the official still had him arrested—after Tell admitted that if he had missed the apple he would have shot the tax collector! Nevertheless, clever Tell managed to escape. Tell's tale is thought to be based on older Norse tales. But to the Swiss, he remains a national hero who struck a blow—or fired a shot—for their independence.

Explore a MEDIEVAL CASTLE

King Arthur's Camelot wasn't a real castle (though Winchester Castle in England has a round table inspired by Arthur's). And medieval castles weren't just fortresses where nobles took shelter from invading enemies or rebelling local folks. In peacetime, a castle was more like a busy office, where the noble collected taxes, heard legal cases, threw crooks in jail, and recruited soldiers. It was also a home for the noble, his family, and the people who served him.

Kitchen
When a noble threw a feast, he served up great gobs of grub. This meant his castle needed a huge kitchen. The ovens in some castle kitchens could roast up to three oxen at once! Some medieval meals for nobles could go on for three hours.

Towers
Round towers offered archers a good view at an approaching enemy. Stairs in a castle tower spiraled up clockwise. This made it easier for defenders to swing their swords if an enemy made it inside the castle and tried to rush up the tower.

Arrow Loops
The trick for an archer is to get off a shot without being shot first. These slits cut into castle walls gave archers the protection they needed to do their jobs.

Dungeon
Hear the word "dungeon" and you probably think: Torture! Pain! Bloodcurdling screams! But in a medieval castle, a dungeon was a place to hold nobles who had been captured in battle. The prisoners could even roam the castle's grounds as they waited for someone to pay money for their release.

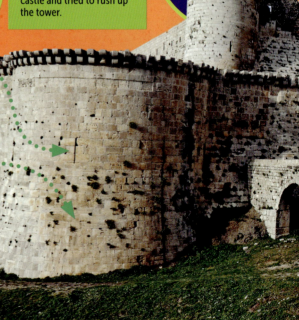

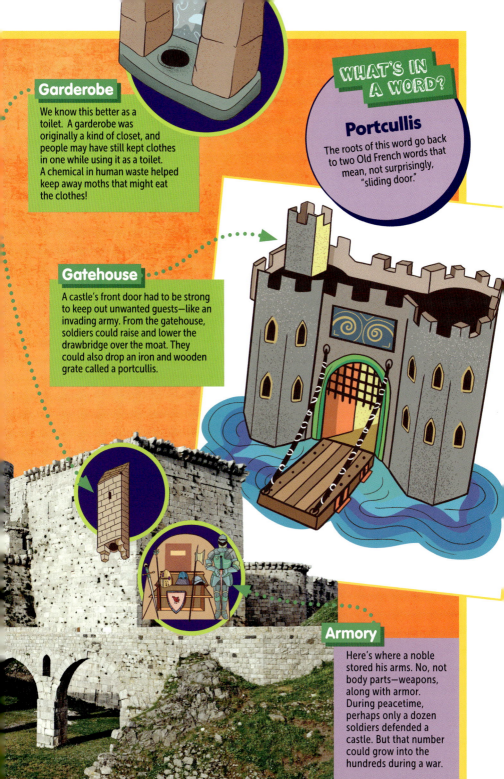

Garderobe

We know this better as a toilet. A garderobe was originally a kind of closet, and people may have still kept clothes in one while using it as a toilet. A chemical in human waste helped keep away moths that might eat the clothes!

WHAT'S IN A WORD?

Portcullis

The roots of this word go back to two Old French words that mean, not surprisingly, "sliding door."

Gatehouse

A castle's front door had to be strong to keep out unwanted guests—like an invading army. From the gatehouse, soldiers could raise and lower the drawbridge over the moat. They could also drop an iron and wooden grate called a portcullis.

Armory

Here's where a noble stored his arms. No, not body parts—weapons, along with armor. During peacetime, perhaps only a dozen soldiers defended a castle. But that number could grow into the hundreds during a war.

139

WHO Lived WHERE

As the Middle Ages went on, existing cities grew and new ones popped up as people moved from the countryside into towns. Here's a look at some of the world's major cities in or around 1300. (Of course, many of these cities shrank in population after the Black Death [see pages 124–127].)

Granada
150,000

Under Muslim rule, this city in southern Spain had become one of the largest in Europe (along with Paris) by 1330. Granada is the home of the Alhambra, a palace and fortress that is one of the greatest examples of Moorish architecture.

Tenochtitlan
200,000

The Aztec founded this city in 1325, and its population soon reached more than 200,000. Read more about the Aztec on pages 150–151.

Cusco
40,000

This city in Peru really started to grow around 1200. It sits more than 11,000 feet (3,450 m) above sea level in the Andes mountain range. It became the capital of the Inca civilization, which ruled large parts of South America during the 15th century (see pages 152–153). At its peak, Cusco had a population of about 40,000, while another 200,000 lived in the surrounding area by the early 16th century.

Timbuktu
15,000

MAP KEY
- Historic city of interest

Present-day countries are shown.

Population numbers can vary based on which source you consult or which expert you ask, because it's hard today to confirm exact figures.

A Great GOLDEN KINGDOM

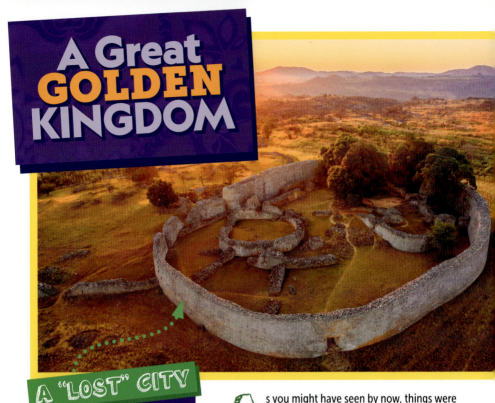

A "LOST" CITY

How do you lose a city? They're usually pretty big. Well, Great Zimbabwe has always been in the same spot. But in the late 19th century Europeans discovered its ruins and thought it was part of some ancient civilization no one had known about before. To them, the city had been "lost" to history. And as these Europeans saw the fine stonework in the city, they couldn't believe it had been crafted by the ancestors of the people who lived there. This idea reflected the prejudice of white Europeans toward the Black Africans. Some people said the city might have been constructed by skilled ancient builders, such as the Phoenicians. Or perhaps it dated to biblical times. Some people even thought it could have been the work of aliens! But archaeologists soon discovered the truth: The Shona people had built it as the capital for their once important kingdom.

As you might have seen by now, things were always changing during the Middle Ages. Empires and dynasties came and went. One city or state rose to power, only to fade away and another take its place. This is what happened in southern Africa, with the kingdom of Zimbabwe and its capital, Great Zimbabwe.

TRADING A TREASURE

Around 1100, a people called the Shona began to build a city on a hill. They farmed and raised cattle, but their ticket to building a new kingdom was gold. Like Mali (see pages 56–57), the kingdom that became Zimbabwe was built on trading this precious metal. It was taken out of rivers and some mines that were 100 feet (30 m) deep. The Shona then traded their gold all over Asia. In return, they received such items as porcelain from China and beads from India. Gold, along with some ivory, went to the port city of Sofala, located on the Indian Ocean. Then, the goods began their journey to distant lands.

AFRICAN EMPIRES 1100 – 1450 ZIMBABWE

A STONE CITY

With their wealth, the Shona chiefs turned the site of Great Zimbabwe into an impressive capital city. Workers hauled granite stones to the hill. On the top, they built homes for the chiefs; religious ceremonies most likely took place there, too. To the south was a walled area known today as the Great Enclosure. The walls are 30 feet (9 m) high, and in some places, four feet (1.2 m) thick. Inside the walls were homes and a stone tower. The tower may have been used to store grain, which the Shona brought to their rulers as a gift. Outside the Great Enclosure were more homes made of stone or brick.

THE END OF THE GOLDEN AGE

Things went well for the Shona in their stone city for a few hundred years ... until they didn't. Away from the city, the farms no longer provided enough food. Several droughts hit the region, the soil lost nutrients, and cattle ate too much of the grass they needed to survive. Trouble came from Europe, too. During the 15th century, Portuguese traders set up shop north of Zimbabwe. They began to control the flow of goods that had once made Zimbabwe so wealthy. By 1450, Great Zimbabwe was empty, and the Shona had moved on to other areas.

WHAT'S IN A WORD?

Zimbabwe

The Shona spoke a language that is one of many grouped together as Bantu. Zimbabwe comes from the Shona words that mean "houses of stone."

MADE in the TRADE

Whether you lived in Africa, Asia, or Europe, odds were you were connected to people on other continents by trade. By land and by sea, merchants used well-known trade routes to bring their goods to eager customers. The Silk Road was part of this system of international trade (see pages 26–27). This map shows some of the other routes merchants took as they bought and sold goods.

TRAVELING FAR USING STARS

When Muslim traders set out on the high seas, the stars helped them get where they were going. Knowing the position of the stars in the sky on any night helped them do that, and a tool called an astrolabe made the job easier. The first astrolabe was made by the ancient Greeks, but Muslim mathematicians and astronomers improved it. An astrolabe had several metal or wood plates stacked together. The plates contained the location of well-known stars, lines of latitude, and other information. Moving the various plates, people could also tell time, and some used astrolabes to try to predict the future based on the positions of stars and planets.

Venice
This city famous for its canals was also one of the great trading centers of the Middle Ages. Its merchants lived in Constantinople and other cities, and they traded directly with parts of China and North Africa. Venice became famous for its ships, and Crusaders sailed from the city by the thousands to reach the Holy Land. Marco Polo started his trip to China from the city, where he and his father and uncle were merchants (see page 107).

Constantinople
With access to two seas and land routes connecting it to East Asia, the Byzantine capital was a center of trade for centuries. Later in the Middle Ages, much of this trade was done by Italian merchants who lived in the city. Special rules favored the Italians, and many grew rich.

Lübeck

Lübeck was one of the German cities that formed the Hanseatic League. During the 13th century, these cities along the Baltic and North Seas were filled with merchants. By joining together, the cities could control trade in the region and beyond. League ships carried textiles, timber, furs, and other goods.

Chinese Routes

When the Mongols ruled China, merchants could get a little rest and relaxation at stations set up along main roads, like the one at Beshbalik in northwest China. The stations were like the Mongols' post offices. Each had riders and horses. When a message came in from another station, a rider took it to the next. Travelers and merchants could stay at the stations, and they didn't have to rough it. Marco Polo wrote that the stations were fit for a king.

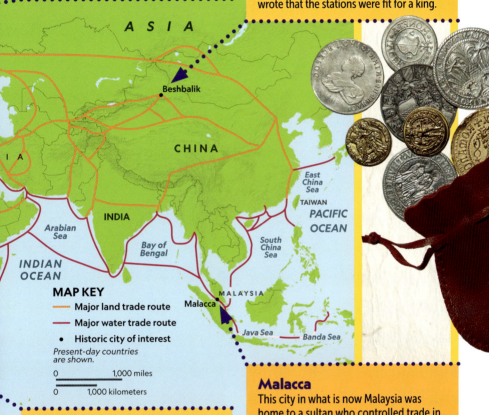

Mombasa

Africa's east coast was a meeting place for Africans, along with Arab, Indian, and Persian traders. Out of that mix came a distinct people known as the Swahili, who spoke a language of the same name. Mombasa, in what is now Kenya, was one of the most important Swahili trading centers on the coast. Goods that passed through the Swahili ports included iron and cotton cloth from India, copper from Persia, and gold from Great Zimbabwe.

Malacca

This city in what is now Malaysia was home to a sultan who controlled trade in the region during the early 15th century. But long before that, the waters there saw ships from many parts of the world pass through with goods. Sailing through the Strait of Malacca gave traders access to East Asia, as it was the most direct water route between India and China. Arabs sailed the straits starting in the eighth century. After the Middle Ages ended, European ships sailed there, too.

145

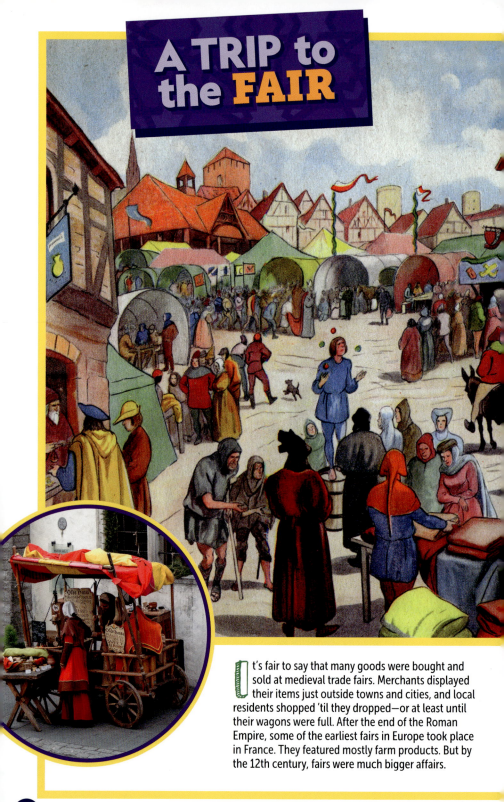

A TRIP to the FAIR

It's fair to say that many goods were bought and sold at medieval trade fairs. Merchants displayed their items just outside towns and cities, and local residents shopped 'til they dropped—or at least until their wagons were full. After the end of the Roman Empire, some of the earliest fairs in Europe took place in France. They featured mostly farm products. But by the 12th century, fairs were much bigger affairs.

WORLDLY WARES

What could you find at a fair? Along with local goods, you might see Chinese silks, furs from Russia, textiles from Belgium, and fine glass from Italy. In the early part of the Middle Ages, buyers traded items of their own to get the goods. Later, paying with coins became more common. Shoppers might travel 20 miles (32 km) on foot to reach a fair, a trip that usually took two days. They made the long journey because they could find better deals there than at local markets. They also scooped up the foreign goods that didn't reach those markets, including foods such as oranges or other fruit that grew only in warm climates.

Not just anyone could host a fair. A town had to get permission from the local lord. Some rulers sought to lure more merchants by letting them travel without paying the usual tolls. Fairs might last a few days or up to several weeks, and they were held at the same spot at the same time of year. In England, fairs were usually held around the feast day for a Roman Catholic saint.

A FLAIR FOR FAIRS

Fairs reached their peak in Europe during the 13th century. And Champagne was the champion of fairs. This region in France was at the center of trade routes that linked northern Europe and the Mediterranean Sea. Merchants from several countries could come to up to six fairs every year, spread out between January and October. Each fair was held in one of four different towns and lasted for weeks. The goods traded included cloth from France and surrounding areas and spices and other expensive goods brought by Italian traders. These fairs were big business until the mid-14th century. War, the Black Death, and new trade routes ended the Champagne fairs.

PARTY TIME!

Trade fairs were not all work and no play. They were festive events, and clowns, dancers, acrobats, and musicians strolled around to entertain the crowds. Gambling sometimes went on, too, which didn't please local church leaders. They looked down on this activity. In England, a popular event was watching wrestling matches. The champ might walk away with a ram for his prize.

Feeling a tad sheepish.

MEDIEVAL EUROPE FAIRS

How to TELL TIME

Got a minute? That's not a question medieval people could easily answer. For one thing, clocks in Europe didn't even keep track of minutes until the 15th century. Throughout the Middle Ages, keeping track of time was a lot harder than pulling out a cell phone or glancing over at a clock on the wall. Here's how you would have told time if you'd lived during the Middle Ages.

THE SUNDIAL

Thanks to the sun, you can see a shadow of yourself. Ancient Egyptians saw that the shadow cast by a stick or rod could help tell time. The shadow moved as the sun moved, and that marked the passage of time. By medieval times, the rod was set in the middle of a disk divided into 12 hours. Of course, the sundial posed some problems. It didn't work at night or on cloudy days. You had to go outside to check the time. And the length of an hour changed during the year: In the winter, the sun shines for a shorter period than in the summer. This meant each hour was shorter in the winter.

RING THOSE BELLS

Instead of looking at a clock, you may have used your ears to gauge time. Church bells rang out to divide the day into different periods. If you were a late sleeper, you wouldn't like the first bells—they rang at 6 a.m. They rang again about every three hours, and they helped tell you what you should be doing—waking up, going to work, going to bed. In some cities, different bells rang to mark different starting times. One London church rang its bells when a market opened. You listened for that bell if you wanted to get the goods before someone else did.

Wakey, wakey!

CLOCKING IN

The ticktock of clocks began with the first mechanical clocks. These first appeared in Europe during the 13th century. Inside each clock, a tiny piece called an escapement moved back and forth at a steady rate. Its movement turned gears that moved the clock's hand. (Yes, just one hand, to keep track of the hours.) And if someone said, "Time's up," they really meant "up": The first mechanical clocks were placed high on church towers. Some of these clocks also tracked the position of the sun and the moon over time.

148

IN THE **11TH** CENTURY, A **CHINESE ENGINEER** BUILT A **WATER CLOCK** THAT WAS **40 FEET (12 M)** TALL.

KEEPING TIME INSIDE

Some devices could help you keep track of time if you were indoors. You might have burned a candle that was marked to show hours or parts of an hour. As the wax melted away, you could see how much time had passed. You also could have used an hourglass filled with sand. When the sand emptied out of the top chamber, you knew a certain amount of time had passed—and that it was time to turn the hourglass over to keep the sand flowing.

WATER YOU WAITING FOR?

Another indoor timekeeper was the water clock. Like sundials, they were used for centuries before the Middle Ages. The basic idea was that water flowed out of one container into another at a steady rate. Lines inside the first container stood for a period of time. You could tell that, say, two hours had passed from when the container was full until the water dropped to the two-hour line. In the Islamic world, inventors came up with fancy water clocks that used moving water to turn gears or ring bells.

All About the AZTEC

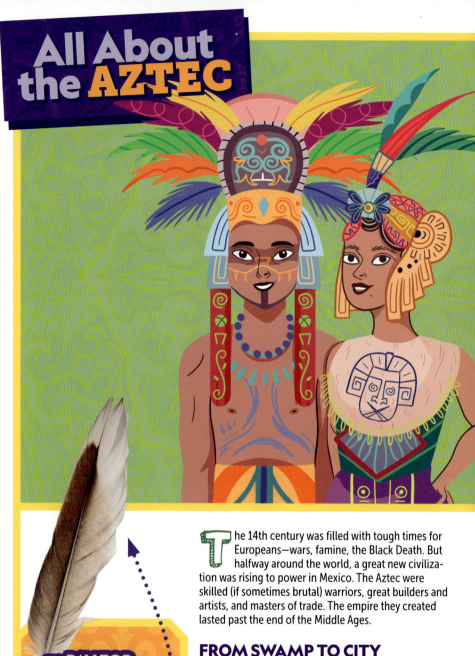

TO PAY FOR ITEMS AT THE MARKET, AZTEC TRADERS USED GOOSE QUILLS FILLED WITH GOLD.

The 14th century was filled with tough times for Europeans—wars, famine, the Black Death. But halfway around the world, a great new civilization was rising to power in Mexico. The Aztec were skilled (if sometimes brutal) warriors, great builders and artists, and masters of trade. The empire they created lasted past the end of the Middle Ages.

FROM SWAMP TO CITY

The Aztec called themselves the Mexica—the root of the name of the modern country of Mexico. In the 13th century, they were said to pass through lands that had been part of the Toltec Empire. The Aztec then found a new home on a swampy island in Lake Texcoco. It was a bleak spot, but the Aztec drained some of the swamps, planted crops, and built a temple to their gods. The island became the city of Tenochtitlan.

From there, the Aztec began to build their empire. First, they made deals with more powerful neighbors, such as the Tepanec, trading goods and marrying into important families. Over time, the Aztec were able to conquer their neighbors and spread their control even farther in central Mexico. On the battlefield, Aztec warriors used clubs covered with razor-sharp blades made from volcanic rocks called obsidian. They also used javelins and a weapon called an atlatl to launch long darts.

AZTEC ACTIVITIES

Off the battlefield, the Aztec grew corn, beans, and other crops on raised islands called chinampas. They built the islands in canals that cut through Tenochtitlan and other towns and villages. The market in their capital city was one of the largest in the medieval world: Up to 60,000 people could cram into the area at one time! The goods bought and sold there included cotton cloth, copper axes, food, spices, cocoa, and feathers from exotic birds.

Religion was an important part of daily life, as it was for people around the world during the Middle Ages. For the Aztec, fighting and defeating the peoples around them was a religious act. They believed they needed to sacrifice their enemies and offer their blood to the Aztec gods. The Aztec also built the Great Pyramid in Tenochtitlan to honor their gods of war and rain.

The Aztec appreciated art, too. Their artists and craftspeople created stone statues, pottery, and jewelry of gold, turquoise, and jade. The Aztec also wrote down their history using colorful images collected in books called codices. And when it was time to play, the Aztec played a version of the ball game that had been played by the Maya and others (see pages 46–47).

TOLTECS

Before the Aztec dominated central Mexico, the Toltecs were the top dogs of the region. They rose to power during the ninth century and built a grand capital called Tula filled with pyramids and other impressive buildings. The Toltec Empire didn't last long, though—it crumbled by the end of the 12th century. But the Toltec influence lived on. When the Aztec traveled through Tula and other parts of the old Toltec lands, they took on some of the Toltec gods as their own.

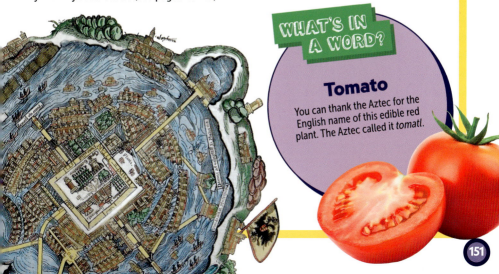

WHAT'S IN A WORD?

Tomato

You can thank the Aztec for the English name of this edible red plant. The Aztec called it *tomatl*.

THE AMERICAS 14TH CENTURY – 16TH CENTURY THE AZTEC

151

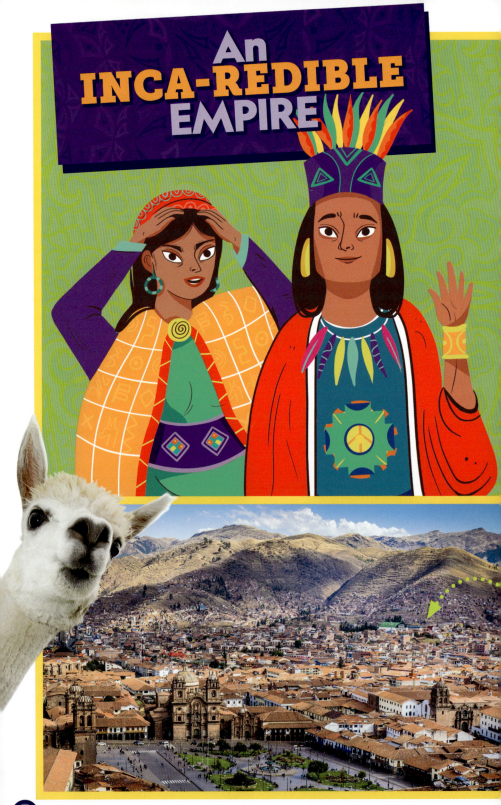

Historians have spilled lots of ink over the Inca—and with good reason! Like the Aztec to their north, the Inca created one of the great civilizations of the Americas. From their capital in Cusco, high in the Andes, the Inca controlled a large part of South America and ruled over about 12 million people. From north to south, their lands stretched for more than 2,000 miles (3,220 km), from what is now Ecuador through much of Chile. Along this stretch, Inca lands went from the Pacific coast, over the Andes, and into part of the Amazon rainforest.

LAST AND STRONGEST

Like the Aztec, the Inca borrowed ideas from earlier peoples in the region. In Peru, the heart of Inca lands, the road to greatness was built by the Wari, the Moche, and especially the Chimu. And there were real roads—the Inca were famous for building two major highways that ran through their land, with other roads branching out from them.

Growing crops wasn't easy in the Andes. Rainfall was limited, and the steep land was hard to farm. So, in the early 1300s, the Inca sought new land. They got it by defeating neighboring people near Cusco, then they just kept going. The empire's greatest growth came during the mid-15th century, under the rule of a leader named Pachacuti. With each Inca victory, the rulers forced their former enemies to fight for them or perform work of some kind.

LIVING GRAND IN THE ANDES

The Inca raised such crops as potatoes, a grain called quinoa, and corn. Farmers also raised llamas and alpacas for their fur, which they turned into clothing. The animals were also used to carry goods. Farmers had to give one-third of everything they produced to their king. To keep track of what the government was owed, royal workers used knotted strings called quipu to record information.

The Inca were also great builders. Pachacuti turned Cusco into a grand city filled with temples and palaces. Outside Cusco, the king built a new city called Machu Picchu. There and at other sites, builders tightly joined stones together—so tight, they didn't need cement or any other kind of "glue" to hold them in place.

Like the Aztec, the Inca made sacrifices to their gods. Victims included enemy chiefs, young Inca, and animals. The sacrifices often took place high in the Andes, and some were held to mark a ruler's big days, such as a birthday or wedding.

THE INCA MADE A FOOD FROM POTATOES CALLED CHUÑO. THEY MASHED, FROZE, AND DRIED THE SPUDS, WHICH REMAINED GOOD TO EAT FOR UP TO 10 YEARS.

I only get better with age.

I WANT MY MUMMY!

Most folks know that ancient Egyptians turned their dead rulers into mummies. But they weren't the only kings given a royal wrapping. Inca rulers were thought to be like gods who lived forever, and their bodies were turned into mummies, too. One citizen was even assigned the job of shooing away flies from the royal mummies! Some people who weren't kings were also mummified after they died.

SPOTLIGHT: THE HEART OF ART

Medieval times are sometimes called the Dark Ages, but there was nothing "dark" about the Middle Ages when it came to art. Skilled artists of all kinds produced great works that are still admired today. Here's a look at a few of them.

DEATH MASK OF PAKAL THE GREAT

If you're curious about masks, you'll learn that the Maya made some real beauties. But these weren't masks for Halloween: Artists made masks of the Maya gods for their rulers, and when the rulers died, a mask was placed on their face. This is the death mask of Pakal the Great, who ruled during the seventh century. It's made of pieces of jade, a gemstone valued by many civilizations across Mexico and Central America. They used it to make jewelry and statues, as well as masks. The Aztec allowed only their royalty to wear jade jewelry.

THE GIFT OF THE MAGI

In 14th-century Italy, Giotto di Bondone created beautiful artwork for several churches. Giotto, as he's called today, had an eye for detail and it showed in his work. His paintings were more realistic than the art created for centuries after the fall of Rome. Giotto painted scenes from the Bible and from the lives of Roman Catholic saints. This painting shows the three wise men bringing gifts to the baby Jesus. His style helped shape the art of the Renaissance that followed the Middle Ages.

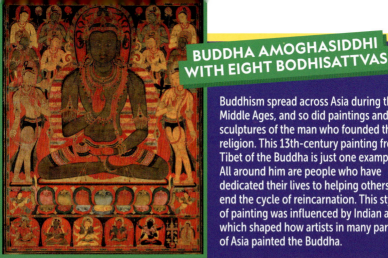

BUDDHA AMOGHASIDDHI WITH EIGHT BODHISATTVAS

Buddhism spread across Asia during the Middle Ages, and so did paintings and sculptures of the man who founded the religion. This 13th-century painting from Tibet of the Buddha is just one example. All around him are people who have dedicated their lives to helping others end the cycle of reincarnation. This style of painting was influenced by Indian art, which shaped how artists in many parts of Asia painted the Buddha.

EQUESTRIAN STATUE

The kingdom of Mali was famous for its gold, but some of its artists worked with a much simpler material. This soldier on his horse is made of terra-cotta, a kind of clay that is heated after the artist shapes it. This sculpture was found near Djenne, an important city since before the Mali kingdom came to power. It dates from around the 13th to the 15th centuries. And it shows how wealthy Mali was. Horses were not native to the area, and the kingdom had to spend a lot of money to feed its steeds.

EWER BASE WITH ZODIAC MEDALLIONS

Everyday items can be works of art, too, as this ewer, or pitcher, shows. Most likely made in Persia during the 13th century, it would have been used to hold water or other liquids. It is missing its neck—with the neck, it was easier to pour out the water. Made of bronze, the ewer also has pieces of silver and copper in it. Around the sides are the signs of the zodiac. Arabic writing on the sides offers blessings to the owner.

NARCISSUS

Roll out the scrolls—that's what plenty of Chinese artists did during the Middle Ages. Drawn on paper or silk, they weren't meant to be on display all the time. Instead, owners unrolled the scrolls in their hands for a short viewing, then rolled them back up and stored them away. This scroll was done on paper and shows the narcissus flower. It was painted during the mid-13th century by Zhao Mengjian, a member of the Southern Song dynasty, which ruled part of China at the time.

WAR Without End

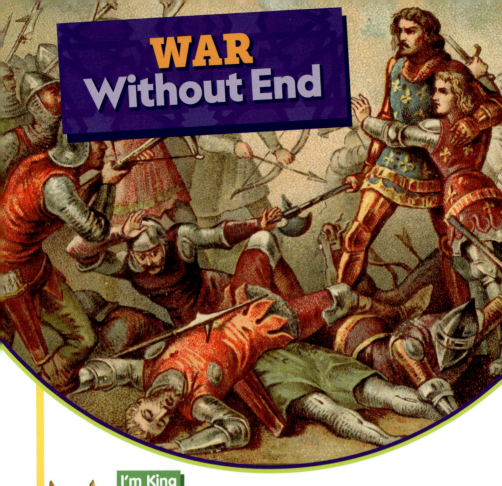

I'm King Phillip VI of France.

Well, to the people of France and England, it sure seemed like an endless war. Known today as the Hundred Years' War, it was certainly more war than they had bargained for. As the name suggests, the kings of the two countries indeed waged war for more than a century (though there were breaks in the fighting). And when the swords finally came down, the map of Europe had changed.

TAKING A STAND OVER LAND

The roots of the war went back centuries. After William the Conqueror won control of England in 1066, the kings who followed him still claimed land in France. By 1337, France's King Phillip VI had had enough. He wanted the English off the European continent and out of what he considered his country. On the other side was King Edward III of England. His mother had ties to the former French king, and Edward thought he should rule France. He proved the point by declaring war on France.

BATTLES BIG AND SMALL

The Hundred Years' War didn't start with much a bang. But by the 1340s, the English were hitting home runs. Their ships destroyed most of a French fleet. Then, land forces came ashore in northwest France and won several key victories. For the first time, the English used cannons. They also made their point with expert use of the longbow. Things were looking really rosy for the English in 1356 when, at the Battle of Poitiers, they captured France's new king, John II. This led the French to give up their claim to lands in France that the English controlled.

FRANCE STRIKES BACK

The peace didn't last, however. Within both France and England, the peasants were revolting. No, they weren't stirring up feelings of disgust in others—they were rebelling against paying taxes. Then, starting in 1369, the French began to peck away at English control of the lands France wanted. But the English weren't ready to give up. In 1415, led by King Henry V, they defeated the French at the Battle of Agincourt. France's King Charles VI then said that Henry would become king of France when Charles died. But Henry died before could that happen, and the war dragged on. Finally, in 1453, the French were able to drive the English out of France. Only the port city of Calais remained in English hands.

WITNESS TO HISTORY

The Peasant Rebellion in France

"These mischievous people thus assembled without captain or armor robbed ... and slew all gentlemen that they could lay hands on ... and he that did most mischief was most praised with them ..."

—*The Chronicles of Froissart*, mid-14th century

THE CHIVALROUS KNIGHT

The oldest son of King Edward III and one of England's heroes during the Hundred Years' War, Edward of England was nicknamed "the Black Prince" because of the color of his armor. He was considered a model of the chivalrous knight, and he fought in several battles during the first phase of the war. His men captured France's King John II at Poitiers. Legend has it that he was such a good host, he helped John out of his armor and then gave him dinner. For a time, he ruled Aquitaine, part of France the English won during the war. But he never became king of England. The Black Prince died a year before his father.

I'm King Edward III of England.

JOAN Jumps In

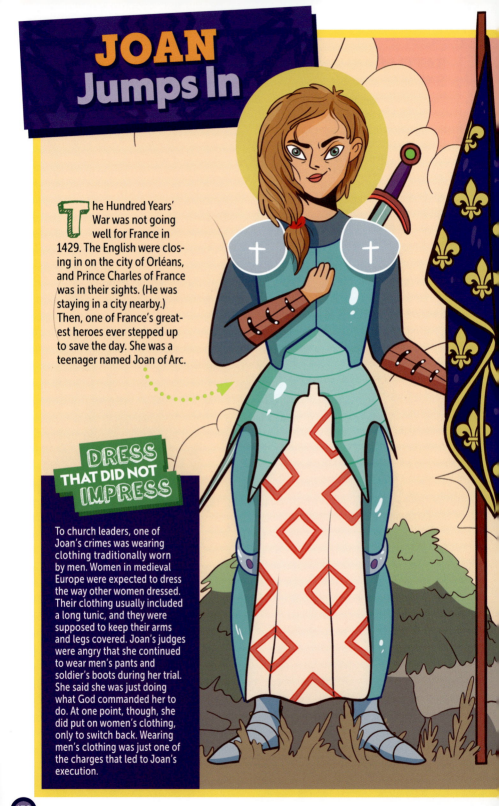

The Hundred Years' War was not going well for France in 1429. The English were closing in on the city of Orléans, and Prince Charles of France was in their sights. (He was staying in a city nearby.) Then, one of France's greatest heroes ever stepped up to save the day. She was a teenager named Joan of Arc.

DRESS THAT DID NOT IMPRESS

To church leaders, one of Joan's crimes was wearing clothing traditionally worn by men. Women in medieval Europe were expected to dress the way other women dressed. Their clothing usually included a long tunic, and they were supposed to keep their arms and legs covered. Joan's judges were angry that she continued to wear men's pants and soldier's boots during her trial. She said she was just doing what God commanded her to do. At one point, though, she did put on women's clothing, only to switch back. Wearing men's clothing was just one of the charges that led to Joan's execution.

HEAVENLY HELP

Joan was the daughter of peasant farmers, but she claimed she had a special gift. She said saints talked to her, and now they wanted her to protect Charles so he could become king. This meant halting the English advance on Orléans. Meeting with Charles, she persuaded him to let her take French forces to stop the English. With nothing to lose, Charles said yes.

MAID WITH A BLADE

Joan called herself *la Pucelle*—"the maiden." She showed she meant business when she put on armor and led troops into Orléans. Under Joan's command, they were able to end a months-long siege of the city. But Joan was just getting started. Her army continued moving north, taking forts under English control. Her goal was the city of Reims, where French kings were crowned. When the city came back under French control, Joan sent word to Prince Charles. He should come to Reims and be crowned king. When the ceremony took place, Joan stood next to the new king.

A FIERY END

By now, Joan was England's Public Enemy Number One. The English got their hands on her after she was captured by French soldiers who were friendly with the English. The English arranged for her to go on trial in a church court, where she was accused of being a witch and breaking rules of the Roman Catholic Church. Joan declared that she was just obeying God's orders. No matter what she said, though, she was doomed. The English wanted her gone, and the court found Joan guilty. She was burned at the stake in Rouen, France, on May 30, 1431.

A SAINTLY HERO

Joan's bravery inspired many French to fight harder against the English. The French ended up driving out their enemy, except in the port city of Calais. Several years after the Hundred Years' War ended, Catholic leaders realized that the court had made a mistake in finding Joan guilty. Ultimately, in 1920, Joan was canonized (declared a saint) by the Roman Catholic Church. And in France today, festivals are held in her honor.

MEDIEVAL EUROPE C. 1412 – 1431 JOAN OF ARC

159

SPOTLIGHT: DO THE CRIME, DO THE TIME

As Joan of Arc's case showed, medieval Europeans could be charged with crimes by church officials. They could also be tried in courts run by public officials. Here's a look at crime and punishment during the Middle Ages in Europe.

"BAD" BELIEFS

One of Joan's crimes was heresy, which was believing something that went against church teachings. Church leaders took these beliefs seriously—so seriously, they might use torture to find out who was a heretic. One medieval torture device was the rack: It stretched a person's arms and legs until they popped out of joint. Gulp. And some people who refused to give up their "bad" ideas met the same fate as Joan—they were burned at the stake. In Spain, after the Middle Ages ended, Roman Catholic leaders there also sought out heretics. They focused on Jews and Muslims who pretended to be Christians but who still secretly practiced their true faith.

IN LATE 12TH-CENTURY **ENGLAND**, ABOUT **ONE-THIRD** OF THE COUNTRY WAS CONSIDERED THE **KING'S FOREST**, AND NO ONE COULD USE IT **WITHOUT HIS PERMISSION.**

160

MY LAND, MY RULES

Medieval kings often claimed lots of land as their own and said it was off-limits to their subjects. Forest laws in France and England said that all the resources in a forest, including its animals, belonged to the king. And sometimes the "forest" included nearby villages, too. In England, someone caught hunting in the king's forest or chopping down a tree for firewood usually paid a fine. But some of these forest criminals lost a limb as punishment for their crime. Today in some English towns, officials are still chosen to watch over the forests.

THE GANG'S ALL HERE

Fourteenth-century England had its share of criminal gangs. Armed gangs might hold up travelers, or even lay siege to a whole town. Who were some of a gang's bad guys? Well, at times, they were knights, or even nobles who could use their money—or their swords—to persuade a judge to let them go if they were caught. One gang leader named Malcolm Musard was a "hired gun"—he led a gang hired to threaten the enemy of a local priest. And sometimes, crime was a family affair: Entire families were known to go out together to rob their neighbors' homes!

A TRICKY TRIAL

In medieval courts, saying you were innocent was all well and good. But how did you prove it? One way was by a "trial by ordeal." The problem was you could win your case and still lose big. In one kind of trial by ordeal, the accused had to hold a glowing-hot piece of iron while walking a short distance. If the accused's hands healed in three days, they were innocent. Another trial by ordeal left the accused person all wet, and usually dead. The alleged criminal was tied up and thrown into water. People thought that a guilty person would float, because the water would reject an evil person. If the accused were innocent, they would sink—but most likely drown.

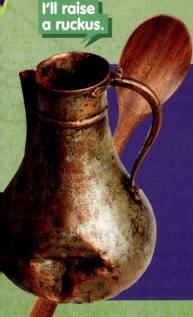

I'll raise a ruckus.

ALARMING ACTION

Ever hear that someone has raised a hue and cry? Today, it means someone has spoken out about some "bad" act. In medieval England, folks were supposed to raise a hue and cry if they saw someone breaking the law. And they didn't just yell, "Stop, thief!" The people were supposed to make as much noise as they could to let their neighbors know a criminal was on the loose. This included banging on pots and knocking on doors. Then, like a posse, the whole neighborhood tracked down the lawbreaker. If someone didn't raise the hue and cry, they could be arrested for not doing their duty. But making a racket when someone hadn't committed a crime was a bad idea. The crier might find themselves crying, because they would have to pay a fine.

161

SPOTLIGHT: MYTHS, MAGIC, and MONSTERS

I like a little mystery.

Zombies and sea monsters and witches, oh my! To many medieval people, all these things were real—and a real threat to humans. Now, the zombies weren't the brain-eating bunch in today's movies; they were just people who wouldn't go away once they died. And one supposed sea monster might have been a real sea beast that someone's imagination made larger than life. Still, people across the Middle Ages believed in things we could call superstitions or myths.

BIG BEASTS OF THE SEA

One Middle Ages myth is still alive and well today: that a giant sea monster lives in Scotland's Loch Ness. "Nessie," as the beast is known, first appeared in a biography of a Christian missionary named St. Columba. The saint is said to have used holy powers to save a man from Nessie's attack. Across Europe, sailors fretted about another vicious sea monster, the Kraken. By some reports, it was one mile (1.6 km) long and could easily eat a ship's entire crew. Today, some scientists think the Kraken was actually a giant squid that in sailors' imaginations was a terrible beast.

WHAT'S IN A WORD?

Genie
The Arabic word for "demons" is *jinni*. That's the source of the English word for a magical wish-granter: "genie."

MAGICAL SCIENCE

Since ancient times, some people thought they could devise a way to turn cheap metals into gold. Or that they could create a medicine that would allow people to live forever. The work that went on in pursuit of these goals was called alchemy. In the Middle Ages, alchemists in Europe and Asia kept right on trying. They sometimes used code to write down their findings, so others wouldn't learn their secrets. And some recipes called for a very common liquid—human pee! Along the way, some alchemists carried out experiments that shaped the development of a real science: chemistry.

WITCH WAYS

Did your milk turn sour for no reason? Did a mysterious illness strike down a loved one? Were your crops ruined by a freak storm? Maybe it was all the devil's work. That's how some people in the Middle Ages explained why bad things happened. And helping the devil do his dirty deeds were people called witches or sorcerers. People did not doubt that witches used black magic to cause harm by casting spells or brewing deadly potions. By the end of the Middle Ages, the Roman Catholic Church was hunting down people wrongfully accused of being witches or sorcerers.

THE DEAD LIVE

Some people just didn't know when to stay in the ground—at least that's what some medieval Europeans thought. They believed some dead people returned to Earth, either to torment the living or to tell their loved ones to stop committing sins. Witches or demons were sometimes said to have had a hand in raising the dead.

THAT'S THE SPIRIT!

Many people of the Middle Ages believed that everything in nature had a living spirit inside it. These spirits sometimes took a visible shape, and in Europe, they were called fairies, sprites, and nymphs. Some of the spirits were helpful, but others were evil. In some stories, fairies carry away living people to a distant fairyland. If the humans eat or drink anything there, they can never return to Earth.

163

TALE
Me More

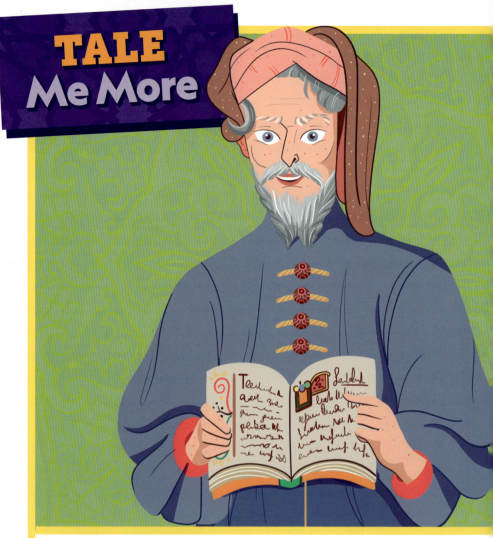

Just horsin' around.

If magic and witchcraft were all around, it's not surprising that they ended up in stories and poems. And perhaps the best known medieval stories still read today are Geoffrey Chaucer's *Canterbury Tales*.

A ROYAL SERVANT

Chaucer's life makes for a great tale itself. He was born around 1340 in London. As a young man, he fought in the Hundred Years' War. He was captured by the French, and England's King Edward III paid for his release. Chaucer became part of the king's court, and later he traveled as a diplomat to several countries, including Italy. For a brief time, he served in Parliament, the government body that makes laws for England.

WELL-READ WRITER

Growing up, Chaucer learned French, and he often read poems written in that language. He later learned some Italian, too. When he began writing his own poetry, Chaucer first focused on courtly love. One of his best, early poems marked the death of the wife of one of King Edward III's sons, John of Gaunt. During the 1370s, on his travels to Italy, Chaucer read the works of Giovanni Boccaccio (see page 109). The Italian's masterpiece influenced Chaucer's greatest work, *The Canterbury Tales*.

A WORLD OF COLORFUL CHARACTERS

Chaucer began working on his long poem around 1387 and continued on it for more than 10 years. In Boccaccio's *Decameron*, a group of travelers takes to the road after the Black Death hits Italy. Along the way, they tell each other stories. In *The Canterbury Tales*, Chaucer's characters do the same thing as they make a pilgrimage to Canterbury, site of a famous cathedral.

In these stories within a story, Chaucer brings together people from all different backgrounds, including a knight, a monk, a merchant, a miller, a nun, and more. The tales the travelers tell take many forms. Some are funny, some are serious, and some poke fun at the Roman Catholic Church. One of the most famous stories is the Nun's Priest's Tale. The priest tells an allegory—he uses animals instead of people as his characters. In the story, a fox praises the singing of a rooster's father. When the rooster begins to crow himself, the fox sinks his teeth into him and carries him off. Several people and other animals begin to chase after the fox, and the rooster persuades the thief to yell at the chasers. But as soon as the fox opens his mouth, the rooster is able to escape. The happy ending comes with a message: Don't listen to people who flatter you.

Chaucer died in 1400. *The Canterbury Tales* was not done yet, but he had written enough of it to please readers of his day and throughout the centuries since.

A DIFFERENT KIND OF ENGLISH

Most people today can't read *The Canterbury Tales* the way Chaucer wrote them. That's because English has changed quite a bit over the centuries. Chaucer wrote in what's called Middle English, because it came after Old English and before our modern English. Here's a look at part of the Nun's Priest's Tale, showing what Chaucer originally wrote and how it would be written today:

This sely wydwe and eek hir doghtres two
Herden thise hennes crie and maken wo,
And out at dores stirten they anon,

This poor widow and also her two daughters
Heard these hens cry and make woe,
And quickly they ran outside.

MEDIEVAL EUROPE C. 1342 – 1400 CHAUCER

SPOTLIGHT: MAKING BEAUTIFUL MUSIC

People of the Middle Ages may not have had smartphones or Bluetooth speakers, but they still enjoyed their tunes. Music could be heard during religious ceremonies, in the homes of nobles, and at festivals and fairs. In Europe, starting with the reign of Charlemagne, music was one of the seven areas of knowledge that educated people were expected to know. Without skipping a beat, here's a closer look at medieval music.

A NOTABLE NOTEMAKER

If you've ever sung "Do, re, mi," you can thank an Italian monk named Guido D'Arezzo. Medieval singers certainly thanked him, as his work made it easier to learn a new tune. Working in the early 11th century, he came up with the system of lines, called a staff, that is still used today to write down musical notes. He also came up with the syllables that stand for the seven notes in the musical scale—which are today's do, re, me, fa, sol, la, ti. Some of these ideas were already being used, but D'Arezzo expanded on them and wrote them down in several books. Later, European musicians put them to use. Unlike some musical scholars, D'Arezzo didn't want to write grand theories—he wanted to find an easier way for choirs to learn new songs for church services.

A MUSICAL NOD TO GOD

In Europe and parts of Asia and Africa, you were likely to hear music during religious ceremonies. A lot of the music written down during the Middle Ages was used for religious services. Many of the "songs" were really chants—prayers said by a group of people in a musical way, but with no instruments accompanying them. Instruments became more common in religious music later during the Middle Ages. In Roman Catholic services, the choirs who chanted were always men or boys.

166

THE MUSLIM INFLUENCE

Many of the ideas about music from ancient times were lost in Europe after the fall of Rome. Europeans should sing the praises of Muslim musicians for helping them make better tunes. The Muslims had a flair for making new stringed instruments, some of which were models for ones later played in Europe, such as the violin. A musician named Ziryab taught music in Muslim Spain during the ninth century, and he's credited with bringing something called the oud to Europe. This stringed musicmaker was the model for the lute, a popular medieval instrument. A wind instrument called the shawm made its way from Muslim lands to Europe during the Crusades, as well. Similar instruments were played in India and China, too.

MUSIC FOR ALL

Outside of palaces and nobles' homes, peasants enjoyed music, too. Traveling musicians called jongleurs sang and danced in public. At dances and other events, musicians would play drums, bagpipes, flutes, and shawms. Other wandering singers were goliards. In their songs, they made fun of church and government leaders and called for people to enjoy themselves. Unlike church music, not much of the music performed by minstrels, jongleurs, and goliards was written down, so modern listeners don't know what they played.

MARCHING INTO BATTLE

Since ancient times, soldiers sometimes went into battle while musicians banged drums or blew horns. But starting in the 13th century, the Ottoman Turks had whole bands that traveled with the troops. The Turks' Mehterhane is considered the world's first military band. Instruments included drums, cymbals, and wind instruments. The music the band played was supposed to make the Turkish soldiers ready to fight—and perhaps scare the enemy a bit. Centuries later, European nations formed their own military bands. Today, you can see military bands playing in parades, special events, or at some government ceremonies.

ROCKIN' WITH THE ROYALS

As the Middle Ages went on, more music could be heard outside of houses of worship. In Europe, rulers made musicians part of their court. These talented tunesmiths would strike up the band and play during important events, especially when their lord was throwing a big bash. Along with stringed instruments, the musicians might blow into a horn or other wind instruments, or ring bells. Some nobles also became troubadours, writing love poems they set to music (see page 135). They might hire musicians called minstrels to play the songs they wrote.

167

A TURKISH EMPIRE

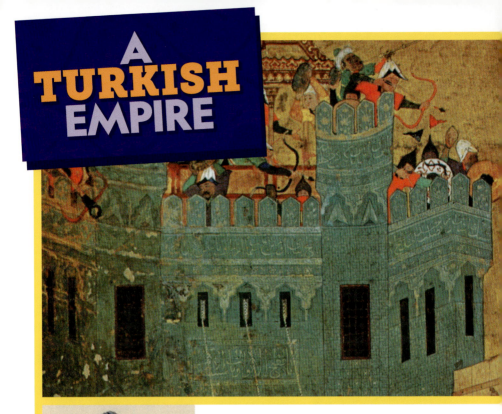

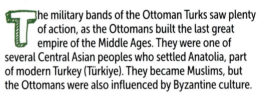

The military bands of the Ottoman Turks saw plenty of action, as the Ottomans built the last great empire of the Middle Ages. They were one of several Central Asian peoples who settled Anatolia, part of modern Turkey (Türkiye). They became Muslims, but the Ottomans were also influenced by Byzantine culture.

OSMAN THE BOSS MAN

The Ottomans got their name from the founder of their ruling dynasty, Osman I. In the 1290s, he ruled a small part of Turkey before setting out to conquer more land. In the decades that followed, he took control of parts of the Byzantine Empire. The sultans who followed Osman continued to expand west into Byzantine lands and east across Turkey.

EUROPE ON THE ROPES

Starting in 1354, the Ottomans made the leap from Asia into Europe. Under the sultan Murad I, they conquered parts of the continent known as the Balkans, taking Bosnia and Serbia. His son Bayezid continued the European conquests into Bulgaria and Hungary. The Ottomans also forced the rulers of other states to become their vassals. But they faced a challenge from

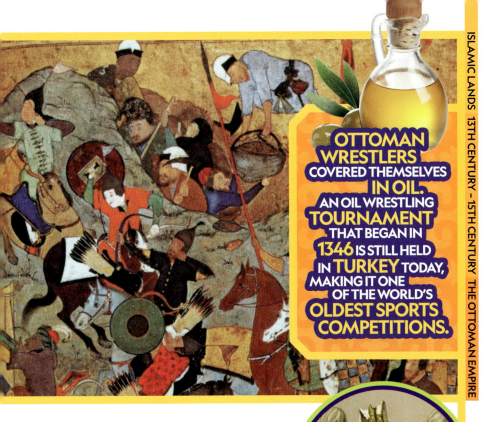

ISLAMIC LANDS 13TH CENTURY – 15TH CENTURY THE OTTOMAN EMPIRE

OTTOMAN WRESTLERS COVERED THEMSELVES IN OIL. AN OIL WRESTLING TOURNAMENT THAT BEGAN IN 1346 IS STILL HELD IN TURKEY TODAY, MAKING IT ONE OF THE WORLD'S OLDEST SPORTS COMPETITIONS.

a Turkic ruler called Timur the Lame, or Tamerlane, who said he was related to Genghis Khan. During the last decades of the 14th century, he attacked the Ottomans, Mongols, and anyone else who stood in his way. After his death in 1405, though, the Ottomans were able to regain their lost lands.

OTTOMAN RULE

Although they were devoted Muslims, the Ottomans didn't force their subjects to accept Islam. And they placed religious leaders under their control. To run their empire, the Ottomans relied greatly on enslaved people. Many served in the army, but some received the same education as the sultans' sons—and were later able to win positions in the government.

THE BIG VICTORY

Through the 1400s, the Ottomans built up their navy so they could challenge European navies in the Mediterranean. Then, in 1453, they seized the city of Constantinople, marking the official end of the Byzantine Empire. The Ottomans renamed the city Istanbul. The only empire that still traced its roots to Rome had come to an end.

THE SULTAN'S SPECIAL SOLDIERS

The Turkish sultans had a special group of warriors devoted to serving them. The members of this force were former Christians and were called Janissaries. The name came from a Turkish word meaning "new soldier." The Janissaries first served as bodyguards for the sultans, then they became the top soldiers in the Ottomans' military forces. They took part in sieges and were the first Ottoman soldiers to use guns in battle. The Janissaries served the sultans until the 19th century.

THE WORLD at the End of the MIDDLE AGES

England
1471 William Caxton prints the first book in English.

Granada, Spain
1492 The last Muslim state in Spain surrenders to the country's Roman Catholic rulers.

MAP KEY
- Historic city of interest
- Area of interest

Present-day countries are shown.

0 — 2,000 miles
0 — 2,000 kilometers

Tenochtitlan, Mexico
c. 1450 The Aztec continue to expand their main temple in their capital city.

Peru
c. 1470 The Inca extend their empire by defeating the Chimu.

Songhai, West Africa
1493 Muhammad I Askia takes control of the Songhai Empire and strengthens it.

170

By some measures, the Middle Ages ended with the fall of Constantinople to the Ottoman Turks. Some historians say the end came a little later, by the end of the 15th century. What was happening elsewhere the world in 1453 and in the years immediately after? Let's see some examples of who was doing what where.

Greenland
1450 One of the large Norse settlements here ends and others disappear before the end of the century.

Florence
c. 1450 Florence becomes the center of the emerging Renaissance in Italy.

Kyoto, Japan
1467 A war begins that leaves much of Japan's capital destroyed and weakens the power of the shogun.

Northern Nigeria
1463–1499 The kingdom of Kano sees economic and cultural gains under Muhammad Rumfa.

Constantinople/Istanbul
1453 The Turks convert Hagia Sophia into a mosque.

A NEW AGE

PRESSING AHEAD

At the end of the Middle Ages, German goldsmith Johannes Gutenberg had *gut* news: He had improved on the printing methods first introduced in China hundreds of years before (see page 72). Gutenberg made movable type out of metal, then put the type into wooden frames. The letters were inked and then pressed on paper. In 1455, Gutenberg printed several copies of the Bible. His printing press then spread across Europe. Writers now had an easier way to share their ideas with greater numbers of people. With more reading material available, more people began to learn how to read. Gutenberg's press has been called one of the greatest inventions ever. This gift from the Middle Ages helped create the modern world.

WHAT'S IN A WORD?

Renaissance
This French word means "rebirth." The Renaissance marked the rebirth, or rediscovery, of the best thought from ancient times.

So, the Middle Ages came to an end. But it wasn't like someone threw a switch and everything from the previous 1,000 years changed overnight. In parts of Europe, especially in the countryside, medieval ways of life lasted for another few hundred years. But in some European cities, new art and ideas had already grabbed hold. They would form the foundation of the next great phase of European history: the Renaissance.

172

LOOKING BACK, MOVING FORWARD

Starting in the 14th century, scholars and artists in Italy began to study what the ancient Greeks and Romans had created. These old ideas led to new ways of looking at the world. For some people, the teachings of ancient thinkers became more important than what saints had to say about how to live. In general, scholars were more willing to challenge the power of the Roman Catholic Church. They wanted to put people and their interests at the center of their studies. This new approach to learning and living was called humanism.

In the arts, poets began to copy the style of the ancient writers, though many stopped writing in Latin and used their native tongue. Painters like Giotto focused more on showing human emotions than simply giving glory to God. Architects were inspired by the great buildings of ancient Rome. Learning about the best of the ancient world got a boost after Constantinople fell: Byzantine scholars had been studying the old ways for centuries. As they fled to western Europe for safety, they brought their knowledge with them.

PEOPLE AND IDEAS ON THE MOVE

The thinking that shaped the Renaissance didn't stay in Italy. Across Europe, scientists and scholars studied humans and the natural world around them, which led to new ideas in science, such as the notion that Earth moves around the sun. Since ancient times, scholars in Europe had incorrectly thought that the sun moved around Earth. Research based in part on science done in the Muslim world helped set things right (see page 97).

The Renaissance also saw a great increase in world exploration, done in large part by European sailors. First the Portuguese and then others built better ships and found new ways to navigate, letting them cross the Atlantic and Pacific Oceans. European leaders wanted to trade with Asia, Africa, and then the Americas. At times, though, they used their better military weapons to simply take what they wanted and enslave the people they met.

GO WITH THE FLO-RENCE

While great thinkers and artists lived in many 15th-century Italian cities, Florence was the first hot spot of the Renaissance. It grew rich from trade of luxury items, such as silk and jewelry. With their wealth, powerful merchant and banking families controlled the city. The most powerful of all was the Medici family, who ran Florence for much of the century. Sometimes they used their money to hire killers to knock off their political rivals. The power-hungry family, however, also saw value in the arts. They hired artists of all kinds to create works that remain masterpieces of the Renaissance. Some of the great artists who lived and worked in the city included Leonardo da Vinci, Michelangelo, and Raphael.

173

GLOSSARY

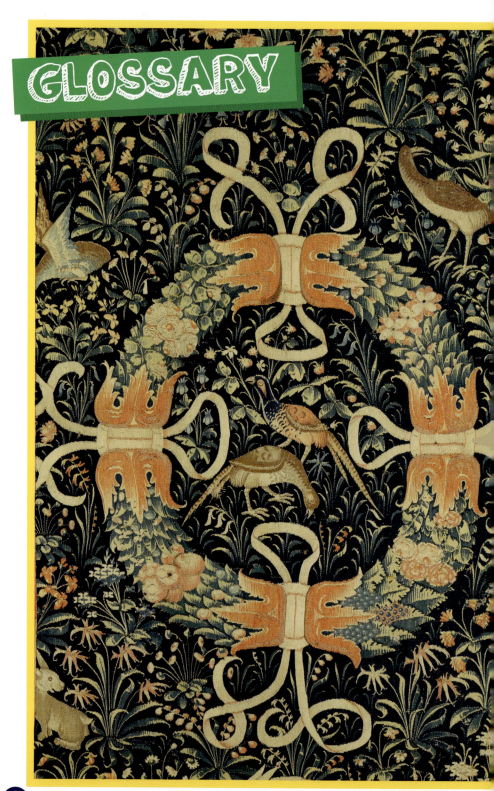

adobe
a building material of dried mud and straw

animism
the belief that all things in nature have souls

apprentice
a young person who learns a craft by living with someone who already knows the craft

archaeologists
scientists who uncover and study items from the past that reveal how people once lived

archers
soldiers who use bows and arrows

armorers
people who make weapons and armor

bacterium
a tiny organism found in other living things; some are helpful, while others cause disease

bishop
in the Christian faiths, an official with more power than a priest

caliph
a Muslim ruler of the Middle Ages

caravans
groups of people and their wagons that travel together over long distances

catapults
wooden machines used in war to fire heavy objects over walls

cathedral
a church where a bishop says Mass

characters
symbols, such as letters, used to write down ideas

domesticate
to take a wild crop or animal and begin to raise it for human benefit

drought
a long period with little or no rain

dynasty
members of the same family who rule over a land, one after the other

empire
different states or territories under the command of one ruler

equinox
a time twice a year, in March and September, when day and night are about the same length

famine
a severe shortage of food, often caused by natural disasters like drought

heretic
a person who rejects the teaching of a religion

illuminator
a person who drew art in medieval manuscripts

latitude
imaginary lines parallel to the Equator that circle Earth, and are used to find locations on the planet

missionaries
people who travel to spread their religion's teachings

Moorish
relating to the Muslims from North Africa who ruled Spain for centuries

New Testament
in the Christian Bible, the writings about Jesus Christ and his teachings

nomads
people who move from place to place to find food for themselves and their animals

nutrients
chemicals that plants, animals, and people need to live

Old Testament
in the Christian Bible, a collection of writing about ancient Jewish history and beliefs

order
groups of monks or nuns who follow the same set of rules

parliament
a government body that makes laws for a country

pestilence
a deadly disease that affects many people

philosophy
the study of the nature of such things as art, religion, and human activity

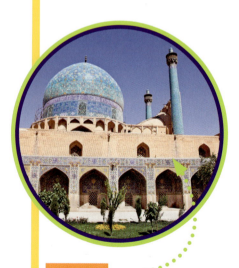

mosque
a building where Islamic religious services are held and a center for learning

pope
the head of the Roman Catholic Church

prejudice
strong like or dislike of a particular group of people because of their race, religion, or ethnic background

prophet
a person who knows directly the will of a god and shares it with others

purgatory
in Roman Catholic teachings, a place where the souls of the dead go if they are not good enough to go directly to heaven but not bad enough to go to hell

realm
the land ruled by a king or queen

reign
to rule over a country, or the length of time one ruler is in power

Renaissance
period near end of Middle Ages from about 1300 to 1600 known for great art and learning

republic
a form of government in which people elect their leaders

sacrifice
item left to honor gods, or the act of leaving them

shamans
in some religions, people thought to communicate with spirits who can heal the sick

siege
the surrounding of a city or castle by a military to force those inside to surrender

thatched
made of straw or other plants woven together

Turkic
related to different peoples who lived in Central Asia, spoke related languages, and settled across western Asia and parts of Europe

vassal
a person who owes loyalty to a more powerful person

INTERVIEW: PETER BROWN

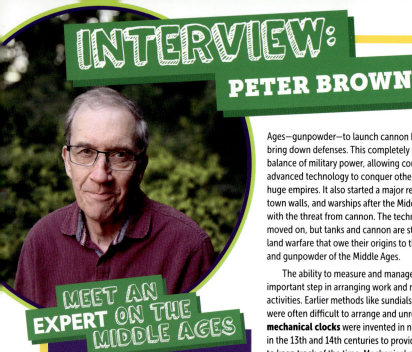

MEET AN EXPERT ON THE MIDDLE AGES

Peter Brown studied archaeology at the University of Leicester, in the same department that later discovered the remains of King Richard III in a parking lot. He is currently researching material for several books, including an unusual castle and the maritime history of his home city.

Why did you want to study medieval history?

I was born in Wales, which has more castles for its size than any other country. So I grew up fascinated by the famous castles (like Chepstow and Caerphilly) that were near to my home. I still love to visit them when I can. My first job was as an archaeologist, and I later specialized in work on protected monuments. That meant lots of work on castles and abbeys from the Middle Ages, which gave me the chance to specialize my interests more.

What ideas or inventions from the Middle Ages are still important today?

Originating in China, blast furnaces were being made across Europe by the end of the Middle Ages, with their most important early use being casting iron cannons. They were able to use another Chinese invention of the Middle Ages—gunpowder—to launch cannon balls that could bring down defenses. This completely changed the balance of military power, allowing countries with advanced technology to conquer others and set up huge empires. It also started a major redesign of castles, town walls, and warships after the Middle Ages, to deal with the threat from cannon. The technology has moved on, but tanks and cannon are still key parts of land warfare that owe their origins to the blast furnaces and gunpowder of the Middle Ages.

The ability to measure and manage time was an important step in arranging work and many other daily activities. Earlier methods like sundials and water clocks were often difficult to arrange and unreliable, and **mechanical clocks** were invented in northern Europe in the 13th and 14th centuries to provide a reliable way to keep track of the time. Mechanical clocks (and later watches) were the common way to measure time until the later 20th century, but they have largely been replaced by digital technology that is cheaper, lighter, and more convenient.

There is some evidence that crude magnifying glasses were used in Greek and Roman times, but the first references to proper **eyeglasses** appeared in the 13th century in Italy and England. These refer to monks, who were among the few people who could read and write then, and who used the glasses to correct their vision and enlarge small images. There are a few paintings from the late Middle Ages that show monks reading with eyeglasses that are set in a frame just like our glasses today. The main difference is that they didn't have arms over the ears and were held on by hand or balanced on the nose. It is estimated that over half of the world's population uses eyeglasses today—and it all started in the Middle Ages!

Public libraries were an invention of the Middle Ages that are still common today. Libraries date back over 2,000 years, but they were only used by specialist researchers and were often attached to religious centers or royal courts. It wasn't until

around 1000 C.E. that the first library appeared that was open to the public. That was called the House of Knowledge and was at Cairo in Egypt.

If you could name three important figures from the time period, who would you choose and why?

This is difficult as there are many choices!

As the Byzantine emperor in the seventh century, **Justinian** did much to restore the decaying Roman empire and re-create it on new footings. He oversaw military conquests, reformed trade and prosperity, and redeveloped Constantinople (now Istanbul) as the world's largest city. He oversaw the building of the church of Hagia Sophia, which remains one of the greatest ancient buildings, and a worthy legacy on its own.

The **Prophet Muhammad** rates as one of the most important figures in world history, and although popularly known as a religious leader, he was also a political and military leader. His achievements were amazing, particularly given his childhood as an orphan. His religious preaching only started when he was over 40, yet by the time he died at 62 he had established Islam as a new religion, attracted many thousands of loyal followers, and conquered most of Arabia. Despite some disagreements over his successor, his followers conquered a huge area in the next 100 years, covering the Middle East, parts of central Asia, all north Africa and even Spain. Today, Muhammad is revered by over one and a half billion followers of his religion.

Look at a map of the Mongol Empire's greatest area, and it still amazes that it really happened in the 12th and 13th centuries. **Genghis Khan** united the Mongolian nomadic tribes and created a fearsome army that made huge conquests and developed superb fighting skills, even incorporating Chinese engineers into the army. Genghis achieved much before he died, but he also set the scene for his descendants to conquer a massive area that included China and Persia, and extended westward to the Holy Land and into Europe as far as Austria. He was not the first leader of Asian nomads to build an empire, but the sheer scale of the operations is amazing. The Mongols also introduced successful ways of managing their conquered territories, supporting their allies, and using advanced systems of communication. Genghis Khan is one of the best known figures in world history, even after 800 years.

In the book, we talked a little about life for kids in the Middle Ages. What were some of the best and worst parts about being a kid at that time?

Life was hard for kids in the Middle Ages. Many didn't survive birth or died while still young, due to diseases or shortages of medical knowledge and care. Those that did survive didn't have the luxuries we enjoy today, and only the wealthy children received an education so they could read and write. Kids also needed to help the family with chores, such as helping in the fields or around the house, because families often provided everything for themselves, rather than using shops as we do today.

Having said that, it wasn't all work, and kids had time to play with their family and friends. Toys were usually handmade rather than bought, using simple wooden things like dolls, blocks and spinning tops. Any carpenter nearby could make these. We also know that in Europe in the Middle Ages there were 'ball games' played—probably using balls made from animal skin—so some kids might have played ball games as well.

As most children couldn't read, stories were passed on by someone telling them to the kids. Other games—of course—didn't need toys, and kids probably played the same games as today, like dressing up, role play, and hide-and-seek. Unfortunately, we don't know much about this because the records and pictures from the Middle Ages rarely tell us about life for kids then.

If it were possible to time travel, would you go back to live in that era?

I would love to see the reality of medieval life—with all its struggles—despite the lack of hygiene! Historians and archaeologists try their best to understand what life was really like in earlier times, but there would never be a better way than to go back to see what it was like and to practice the work and life. I suspect that having had that experience you probably wouldn't want to stay there forever though!

TEST YOUR Knowledge

So, now you're a master of all things medieval. Let's see how much you remember about the Middle Ages with another little quiz. Don't worry if you can't remember an answer—you can find it in the book!

1 Scientists and engineers in China invented all these things except _____.

a. rockets
b. windmills
c. movable type
d. gunpowder

2 Which of these was a not a feature of a medieval castle?

a. garderobe
b. arrow loops
c. portcullis
d. trebuchet

3 In its history, the Hagia Sophia has been all these things except ____.

a. a marketplace
b. a museum
c. a mosque
d. a church

④ **In battle, the Mongols sent messages to each other by _____.**

a. shouting across the battlefield
b. waving flags
c. tying messages to trained pigeons
d. beating drums

⑤ **Before going into battle, Viking berserkers were said to _____.**

a. pray to the god Odin
b. bite their shields
c. take off their clothes
d. eat bread made from barley

⑥ **When he visited the Muslim holy city of Mecca, Mansa Musa brought with him _____.**

a. 500 elephants
b. a water clock
c. a ton of gold
d. Chinese porcelain

ANSWERS:

1. **b**—The Persians are thought to have invented the windmill, and Crusaders later took the concept back to Europe.
2. **d**—A trebuchet was a weapon invaders used to try to attack a castle.
3. **a**—Right! Built by Justinian I, this building started as a church before being turned into a mosque at the end of the Middle Ages. Now it's a mosque again, though anyone can enter it to explore its splendor.
4. **b**—You flagged down the right answer! They also lit fires to send signals to each other.
5. **b**—And along with that, some of these warriors were said to take a swing at their own men.
6. **c**—Yes! Mansa Musa ruled the African nation of Mali, which was famous for its gold.

181

Boldface indicates illustrations.

Aachen, Germany 37, **37**
Alchemy 163
Algebra 94, 96, 97
Alighieri, Dante 109, **109**
Anasazi 54
Angkor Wat, Cambodia 87, **87,** 112
Angles (tribe) 35
Animism 74, 105
Apprentices 121, **121,** 130
Arabic numerals 94, 97
Armor
  crusaders 80–81, **80–81**
  samurai 65, **65**
Art and artists 67, 154–155, **154–155,** 173
Arthur (legendary king) 100, 137, 138
Astrolabes 144, **144**
Augustus, Emperor (Roman Empire) 10, 11
Avicenna 97, **97**
Aztec 140, **150,** 150–151, 154, 170

Baghdad, Iraq 35, 96, 105
Barbarians 12
Barons 59, 60, 98–99
Bayeux Tapestry 133, **133**
Benedict of Nursia, Saint 17, **17**
Beowulf (poem) 136
Berserkers 41, **41**
Bible 29, 154, 172
Black Death 109, 123, 124–127, 141, 147, 165
Black Prince 157, **157**
Boccaccio, Giovanni 109, **109,** 165
Bologna, Italy: university 112, **112**
Bookmaking 72, 172

Books 108–109, **108–109;** *see also* Codices; Illuminated manuscripts
Bows and arrows
  composite bows 90, **90**
  crossbows 91, **91**
  longbows 91, **91,** 157
  poison-tipped arrows 103
  used by samurai 63, **63,** 64, **64**
Bread 115, **115,** 121, **121,** 131, **131**
Brown, Peter **178,** 178–179
Bubonic plague 23, 27, 124–127
Buddha 75, 87, 155, **155**
Buddhism
  origin and beliefs 75, 87, 155
  shrines and temples 69, 87, **87,** 112
  spread of 27, 75, 87, 155
Buddhist monks: printing 72
Burial ships 44, **44,** 45
Byzantine Empire 13–15, 21–24, 31, 74, 77, 168–169; *see also* Constantinople

Cahokia, Illinois **50,** 51, **51**
Cairo, Egypt 95, **95,** 112, **112,** 141, 179
Calendars 47, **47,** 96
Caliphates 30
Cannons 73, 91, **91,** 157, 178
The Canterbury Tales (Chaucer) 164–165, **165**
Castles **78,** 85, **85,** 138–139, **138–139,** 178
Catapults 70, 91, **91,** 175
Cathedrals 37, 86–89, **86–89,** 165
Cavalry 90, **90**
Caxton, William 170
Cenotes 48, **48**
Chaco Canyon, New Mexico 55, **55**
Chain mail **80,** 81
Chamber pots 123, **123**
Chariot races 15, **15**
Charlemagne 33–37, **36,** 59, 90, 135
Charles VI, King (France) 157
Charles VII, King (France) 158, 159, **159**
Chaucer, Geoffrey 164–165
Chess **94,** 95
Chichén Itzá, Mexico 48–49, **48–49**

182

Children 120–121, **120–121,** 179
China
    inventions 72–73, **72–73,** 178
    Mongol rule 103, 105, 107, 145
    Song dynasty 70–73, 105, 107, 141, 155, 157
    trade routes 26–27, 145
    Yuan dynasty 107
    see also Hangzhou; Kaifeng
Chivalry 134–135, 157
Chola Empire 66–69
Christianity
    beliefs 29, 74
    missionaries 17
    monks 16–17, **16–17**
    nuns **110,** 110–111, **111**
    origin of 74, 77
    spread of 9, 11, 15, 27, 35, 74
    see also Crusades
Church bells 88, 148, **148**
Cities, major: world map 140–141
City life: western Europe 122–123
Clocks 35, 96, 148–149, **148–149,** 178
Clothing 118–119, **118–119,** 139, 158
Codices 151
Compasses 6, 72–73, 73
Constantine, Emperor (Roman Empire) 11, 14, 15, 74
Constantinople 11, 14–15, 21, 86, 179
    fall of (1453) 86, 91, 169, 171
    plague 23
    population 141
    as trading center 26, 144
    see also Istanbul
Convents 111, **111,** 112, **116,** 121
Cordwainers 131, **131**
Corn **52–53,** 53
Crime and punishment 8, 99, 160–161
Crusades 76–85, **77, 84,** 92–93
Cusco, Peru 140, **140, 152,** 153

D'Arezzo, Guido 166
Death 126–127
Death masks 154, **154**

Decameron (Boccaccio) 109, 165
Delhi, India: population (c. 1300) 141
Desert dwellers 16, 54–55
Diseases 23, 27, 123–127
The Divine Comedy (Alighieri) 109
Dome of the Rock, Jerusalem **76,** 79, 86, **86**
Domesday Book **108–109,** 109
Dublin, Ireland: Vikings 42
Dungeons 138

Edward II, King (England) 133
Edward III, King (England) 156, **157,** 164, 165
Eggplant 38, **38**
Egypt
    Ayyubid dynasty 93
    Black Death 141
    monasteries 16
    wheat and grain 15, 38
    see also Cairo
Egyptians, ancient 47, 148, 153
Eleanor of Aquitaine **82,** 82–83, **83**
Elephants 25, **25,** 35, **35,** 107, 181
England
    Anglo-Saxon burials 45
    forest laws 161
    Norman Conquest 59, 109, 133, 156
    peasant rebellion 157

183

public schools 121
taxes 98–99, 157
Viking raids 9
see also Hundred Years' War; London; Oxford
Enslaved people 12, 41, 169, 173
Erik the Red 43
Eriksson, Leif **42,** 43, 109
Ewers 155, **155**
Eyeglasses 178, **178–179**

Fabrics 118, **118,** 119
Fairs 146–147, **146–147**
Famine 114, 115
Farming 27, **27,** 38–39, **38–39**
Feudalism 58–62
Fez, Morocco: university 112, **112**
Fiefs 58, 60, 61
Firdausi, Abu'l Qasim 108, **108**
Fireworks 72, **72**
Flagellants 126, **126**
Florence, Italy 125, 141, 171, 173
Food
　crops 52–53, **52–53,** 95, **95**
　daily meals 114–115, **114–115**
　feasts 114, 115, 138, **138**
　markets and fairs 131, 147, **147**
Forests 115, 116, **160,** 161
France
　fairs 146, 147
　feudalism 59
　forest laws 161
　peasant rebellion 157
　tournaments 101
　troubadours 135
　see also Hundred Years' War; Normandy; Paris
Frankish kingdom 32–33
Frankish states 78–79, 85

Ganges River, India-Bangladesh 66, 67

Garderobes 139, **139**
Genghis Khan 102, 102–105, 169, 179
Germany 10, 32, 33, 35, 37, 41, 110, 122, 125
Ghana 56–57
Giotto 154, 173
Gokstad ship 44, **44**
Gold **56,** 56–57, 96, **142,** 142–143, 150, 163
Gong farmers 123
Goths 13, 13, 15, 87
Granada, Spain 140, 140, 170
Grapes 38, **38**
Great Zimbabwe, Zimbabwe 141, 142–143, **142–143**
Greek fire 90, **90**
Greenland: Viking settlements 43, 171
Guilds 130
Gunpowder 72, 73, 91, 178
Gutenberg, Johannes 172

Hagia Sophia, Istanbul, Turkey **14,** 22, 86, **86,** 171, 179, **180**
Hangzhou, China 70, 141
Hanseatic League 145
Henry II, King (England) 82, 83
Henry III, King (England) 99, 114
Henry V, King (England) 157
Heresy 160
Hildegard of Bingen **110,** 110–111, **111**
Hinduism
　gods 67, **67,** 87
　origin and beliefs 75

temples **66,** 67, 69, **69,** 87, **87**
Holy Land 76–87, 93, 95, 105, 113, 144, 179
Home remedies 128–129, **128–129**
Horses
    armor 81, **81**
    cavalry 90, **90**
    chariot races 15, **15**
    horseshoes 39, **39**
    large breed 76, **76**
Hospitals 85, 95, **95**
Housing 116–117, **116–117**
Hues and cries 161
Hundred Years' War 156–159, 164
Huns 13, **13**

I

Ibn Rushd 97, **97**
Iceland: Vikings 43, 109
Illuminated manuscripts 18–19, **18–19**
Inca Empire 140, 152–153, 170
India
    Buddhist temples 69, 87, **87**
    Chola Empire 66–67
    Hindu temples **66,** 67, 69, **69**
    musical instruments 45, 167
    numbering system 94
    religions 67, 75
    trade 26, 38, 95, 142, 145
    see also Delhi; Ganges River
Islam
    beliefs 29, 75, 76
    extent of (750): map 31
    impact of 94–95
    origin of 28–29, 75
    spread of 27, 30–31, 75, 94
    see also Crusades
Istanbul, Turkey 11, **14,** 169, 179; *see also* Hagia Sophia
Italy
    ancient Rome 11, 15, 113
    artists 154, 173
    medicine and health 52, 113
    navies 79, **79**
    Renaissance 173
    trade 123, 147
    see also Bologna; Florence; Venice

J

Janissaries 169
Japan 62–63, 106, 107, 108, 171
Jazari, Ibn a-Razzaz al- 96, **96**
Jerusalem **76,** 77–78, 84–86, **86,** 93
Jesters 132–133, **132–133**
Jesus 7, 29, 74, 76, **154**
Joan of Arc **158,** 158–160, **159**
Jobs 12, 52, 69, 123, 130–131
John, King (England) **98,** 98–99
John II, King (France) 157
Jokhang Temple, Lhasa, Tibet 87, **87**
Jousting 25, **25,** 100, **100,** 100–101, **101**
Judaism 29, 74, 86
Justinian, Emperor (Byzantine Empire) **20,** 21–23, 86, 179
Jutes (tribe) 35

K

Kaifeng, China 8
Kamikazes 106
Khanates 105
Khayyam, Omar 96, **96**
Khwarizmi, Muhammad ibn Musa al- 96, 97
Kindi, Abu Yusuf Ya'qub ibn Ishaq -al 96, 97, **97**
Kings and queens: social rank 60
Kivas 55, **55**
Knights
    armor 80–81, **80–81**
    chivalry 134–135, 157
    crusades 77, 78, **84,** 84–85, **85**
    social rank 61
    special orders 84–85
    tournaments 25, 100–101, **100–101**
Krak de Chevaliers (castle), Syria 85, 85
Kraken (sea monster) 162
Kublai Khan 105, 106–107
Kyoto, Japan: war 171

L

Ladoga, Russia 42
Langton, Stephen 99, **99**
Legends 136–137
Leo III, Pope 35
Libraries, public 178–179
Loch Ness monster 162, **162**
London, England 8, 99, 119, 127, 141, 148
Lords and ladies 59, **59**
Louis VII, King (France) 82, 83, **83**
Love, courtly 135
Lübeck, Germany 145
Lyres 45, **45**

M

Machu Picchu, Peru 153
Magna Carta 98–99, **99**
Mahabodhi Temple, Bodh Gaya, India 87, **87**
Malacca, Malaysia 145
Mali, kingdom of 57, 155
Maps
    Byzantine Empire 22
    Charlemagne's empire 36
    extent of Islam (750) 31
    15th-century events 170–171
    major cities (c. 1300) 140–141
    major religions 74–75
    major trade routes 144–145
    Sassanian Empire 24
    Silk Road 26
    Vikings 42–43
Markets 131, 147, 151
Martel, Charles **32,** 33, **33**
Mathematics 94, 96, 97
Maya 46–49, 52, 53, 151, 154, 155
Mecca, Saudi Arabia **28,** 29, **29,** 56, 57
Medicine and health
    barber-surgeons 9
    diseases 23, 27, 123–127
    doctors **79,** 95, 97, 111, 125, 128
    hospitals 85, 95, **95**
    remedies 125, 128–129, **128–129**
Melees 101
Merchants: social rank 60
Mesa Verde, Colorado **54,** 55
Middle English 165
Mississippians 51
Moats 69, 117, **117,** 139, **139**
Mombasa, Kenya 145
Monasteries **16,** 16–18, **18,** 21, 111, 112, 121
Mongol Empire 57, 71, 90, 102–107, 145, 179
Monks **16–17,** 16–19, 21, 72, 85, 178
Mosques **76,** 86, **86,** 112, 171
Mounds 44, **50,** 50–51, **51**
Movable type 72, **72,** 172
Muhammad (prophet) 28–31, 52, 75, 76, 86, 179
Mummies 153
Musa, Mansa 56, **56,** 57
Music 95, 97, 111, 135, 166–167
Myths 136, 137, 162–163

N

Newfoundland, Canada 43, 109
Nigeria: kingdom of Kano 171
Nobles
    clothing **60,** 118, 119
    food 115, 138
    houses 116–117
    social rank 60
Normandy, France 43, 109
Notre Dame Cathedral, Paris, France **86–89,** 87–89

Nuns 58, **110,** 110–111, **111,** 121

Olives 38, **38**
Ottoman Empire 168–169
Ouds 95, **95,** 97, **97,** 167, **167**
Oxen 39, **39,** 58
Oxford, England: university 112, **112**

Pagan beliefs 74
Pakal the Great (Maya ruler) 154, **154**
Paper money 73, **73**
Parchment 18, **18,** 19
Paris, France 113, 123, 125, 130, 131, 141;
 see also Notre Dame Cathedral
Peas 39, 53, **53,** 115
Peasants
 food 53, 115
 houses 117
 music 167
 rebellions 71, 107, 157
 role in society 59
 social rank 61
Persia 24, 95, 103, 105, 137, 145, 179
Peru. see Cusco
Philip VII, King (France) 156, **156**
Pigeons 92, **92**
Pilgrims 79
Pipe organs 89, **89**
Plague 23, 27, 107, 109, 124–127
Plows 27, **27,** 39, **39**
Polo, Marco 9, 107, 144, 145
Potatoes 153, **153**
Printing press 172, **172**
Pueblo people 54, 55
Purple dye 118

Quarantine 127
Quills **18,** 150, **150**
Quran 29, **29**

Rajaraja I, Emperor (Chola Empire) **68,** 68–69
Rashid, Harun al- 35
Religions, major: world map 74–75
Renaissance 6, 171, 172–173
Rice 52, **52,** 70
Richard I, King (England) 82, 83, **83,** 93, 98, **98**
Rockets 73, **73**
Roman Empire: rise and fall of 10–11, 12–13, 14
Russia 10, 26, 41, 42, 105, 147

Sacred sites 86–87, **86–87**
Saladin 83, **92,** 92–93, **93**
Samurai 62–65, **62–65**
Sassanian Empire 24–25, 26, 27, 31
Saxons 35
Scrolls 155, **155**
Sea monsters 162, **162**
Serfs 61, **61**
Seville, Spain: Vikings 43
The Shahnama (Firdausi) 108
Shamans 103, 105
Shikibu, Murasaki 108, **108**
Shiva (Hindu god) 67, **67,** 69
Shoes 122, **122,** 131, **131**
Shoguns 62
Shona 142–143
Siege weapons 91, **91,** 103
Silk 23, **23,** 27, 67, 70, 118, 119, 173
Silk Road 26–27, 144
Smiths 131
Social ranks 60–61, 114, 125
Song dynasty 70–73, 105, 107, 141, 155, 157
The Song of Roland (poem) 135
Songhai Empire 170
Sorghum 53, **53**
Spain
 heretics 160
 invading tribes 13
 Muslim rule 33, 135, 140, 167, 170

the Reconquest 77
see also Granada; Seville
Spices 25, 26, 27, 115, **128,** 147, 151
Spirits 163
Sundials 148, **148,** 178
Syria 16, 21, 30, 31, 77, 85, **85,** 93

T

Tamerlane 169
Tea 70, 71, **71**
Tell, William 137
Tenochtitlan, Mexico 140, 150–151, **151,** 170
Textile industry 131, **131**
Thatched roofs 51, 117, **117, 143**
Theodora, Empress (Byzantine Empire) 20, 21–23
The Thousand and One Nights (folk tales) 137
Tibet
    Buddhist temple 87, **87**
    13th-century painting 155, **155**
Timbuktu, Mali 57, **57,** 112, 140
Timekeeping 148–149
Toltecs 49, 150, 151
Tomatoes 151, **151**
Tournaments 25, 100–101, **100–101**
Toys and games 95, **120,** 121, **121,** 179
Trade fairs 146–147, **146–147**
Trade routes 26–27, 144–145, 147

U

Universities 57, 112–113, **112–113**
Urban II, Pope 77, 79

V

Vandals 13, **13**
Vassals 60, 61, 62, 99, 168
Vellum 18, 19
Venice, Italy 123, 127, 144
Vikings 9, **40,** 40–45, **41,** 74, 109

Warfare: medieval tactics 90–91, 178
Waste, human 123, 139
Water clocks 35, 149, **149,** 178
Weapons 64, **64,** 90–91, **90–91;** *see also* Bows and arrows; Cannons
Wheat 38, **38,** 39, 158
William the Conqueror 59, **59,** 109, 133, 156
Windmills 95, **95**
Wine 38, 128
Witches and sorcerers 163
Women
    clothing 119, 158
    jobs 130, **130,** 131, **131,** 141
    samurai 62, **62**
Women's rights 21, 41, 103
Wrestling 147, 169
Writing systems 37, 41, 46, 47

Y

Yuan dynasty 107

Z

Zhao Mengjian 155
Zimbabwe 142–143, **142–143**
Zoroastrianism 25

PHOTO CREDITS

Illustrations by Carmen Sanchez. Maps and globes by NG Maps.

Front cover (background), javarman/Adobe Stock; back cover (CTR), Alexander Potapov/Adobe Stock; (CTR RT), Num Lpphoto/Shutterstock; 1, pedrosala/Shutterstock; 2-3, scaliger/Adobe Stock; 2 (crown), Maksym Yemelyanov/Adobe Stock; 2 (lords & ladies), Ivy Close Images/Alamy Stock Photo; 3, Maria-Kitaeva/Shutterstock; 4-5 (background), imageBROKER/Alamy Stock Photo; 4 (UP), Pavel Timofeev/Adobe Stock; 4 (LE), swisshippo/Adobe Stock; 4 (CTR LO), Lordprice Collection/Alamy Stock Photo; 4 (LO), Museum of London; 5 (Omar Khayyam), Mohammad Barahouei/Dreamstime; 5 (Quran), akulamatiau/Adobe Stock; 5 (LO LE), Tony Cordoza/Alamy Stock Photo; 5 (RT), Miramiska/Adobe Stock; 6-7, Album/Alamy Stock Photo; 6 (kaleidoscope pattern), bairiki/Adobe Stock; 6 (UP), Heartland Arts/Adobe Stock; 8-9, matorina/Adobe Stock; 8 (CTR), Andrey Burmakin/Shutterstock; 8 (LO), Wirestock/Adobe Stock; 9 (CTR), stoatphoto/Adobe Stock; 9 (LO), Seregam/Shutterstock; 10, Galina Trenina/Adobe Stock; 11, Universal Images Group North America LLC/Alamy Stock Photo; 12, Giancarlo Costa/Bridgeman Images; 13 (coat of arms throughout), Andrey Kuzmin/Shutterstock; 13 (Fleur de Lis texture throughout), Junglebay/Dreamstime; 14 (UP), Sergii Figurnyi/Adobe Stock; 14 (LO), Bridgeman Images; 15 (UP), Bridgeman-Giraudon/Art Resource, NY; 15 (RT), Mustafa/Adobe Stock; 15 (LO), Bridgeman Images; 16, Alexey Devyatov/Shutterstock; 17 (UP), INTERFOTO/Alamy Stock Photo; 17 (CTR), zatletic/Adobe Stock; 17 (LO), patrimonio designs/Adobe Stock; 18-19 (background throughout), fivepointsix/Adobe Stock; 18 (UP), odify260/Adobe Stock; 18 (CTR), Jean Cezard/Adobe Stock; 18 (LO), Rogers Fund, 1998/Metropolitan Museum of Art; 19 (UP), cobracz/Adobe Stock; 19 (CTR), The Cloisters Collection, 1954/Metropolitan Museum of Art; 19 (LO), Peter Horree/Alamy Stock Photo; 21 (UP), tuulijumala/Shutterstock; 21 (LO), Denis Tabler/Adobe Stock; 22, Historia/Shutterstock; 23 (UP), CPA Media Pte Ltd/Alamy Stock Photo; 23 (UP RT), Kal′vān/Adobe Stock; 23 (CTR), Artepics/age fotostock; 24, The Print Collector/Alamy Stock Photo; 25 (UP), Gianni Dagli Orti/Shutterstock; 25 (CTR), Alexeiy/Adobe Stock; 25 (RT), Patryk Kosmider/Adobe Stock; 26 (UP), grafixme/Adobe Stock; 26 (vase), dezign56/Adobe Stock; 26 (scoop and cloves), andriigorulko/Adobe Stock; 26 (ginger), nata777_7/Adobe Stock; 27 (silk textiles), Deanna Laing/Shutterstock; 27 (olive oil), baibaz/Adobe Stock; 27 (ivory tusk), gavran333/Adobe Stock; 27 (LO), Sham-ann/Shutterstock; 28, 29 (UP), Mohd/Adobe Stock; 29 (LO), Vladimir Melnik/Adobe Stock; 29 (LO RT), akulamatiau/Adobe Stock; 30, Heritage Image Partnership Ltd/Alamy Stock Photo; 31 (LE), Gianni Dagli Orti/Shutterstock; 31 (CTR), Peter Horree/Alamy Stock Photo; 32 (background), Pack-Shot/Shutterstock; 32 (UP), 33 (UP), Mary Evans Picture Library; 33 (LO), SPCOLLECTION/Alamy Stock Photo; 35 (LE), Universal History Archive/UIG/Shutterstock; 35 (RT), Kharbine-Tapabor/Shutterstock; 36, Hemis/Alamy Stock Photo; 37 (LE), Alfredo Dagli Orti/Shutterstock; 37 (RT), engel.ac/Adobe Stock; 38-39, The Picture Art Collection/Alamy Stock Photo; 38 (wheat in burlap sack), Evan Lorne/Shutterstock; 38 (wheat ears), Pavel Timofeev/Adobe Stock; 38 (barley), Madlen/Shutterstock; 38 (rye ears), pilotl39/Adobe Stock; 38 (olives), Yeti Studio/Adobe Stock; 38 (grapes), A_Skorobogatova/Adobe Stock; 38 (eggplant in background), Oleg Golovnev/Shutterstock; 38 (eggplant in foreground), atoss/Adobe Stock; 39 (CTR), Lanmas/Alamy Stock Photo; 39 (LO), Anatoliy Sadovskiy/Adobe Stock; 40 (LO), North Wind Picture Archives/Alamy Stock Photo; 40 (rope), Elnur/Adobe Stock; 40 (fire), hugolacasse/Shutterstock; 41 (UP), Print Collector/Getty Images; 41 (LO), Peter Nahum at The Leicester Galleries, London/Bridgeman Images; 42 (LE), Whpics/Dreamstime; 42 (RT), banepetkovic/Adobe Stock; 43 (UP), Album/British Library/Alamy Stock Photo; 43 (LO), Iliuta/Adobe Stock; 44-45, M. Havgar/KHM; 44 (UP), LHismanto/Shutterstock; 44 (LO LE), Adobe Stock; 44 (LO RT), Maria Luisa Cianca/Shutterstock; 45 (UP), Colin Young/Dreamstime; 45 (RT), Maria-Kitaeva/Shutterstock; 45 (RT background), matorina/Adobe Stock; 45 (LO), Zoonar GmbH/Alamy Stock Photo; 46 (UP), DC_Aperture/Shutterstock; 46 (LE), christian vinces/Adobe Stock; 46 (LO), xunantunich/Adobe Stock; 47 (UP), nok3709001/Adobe Stock; 47 (CTR), deborahatl/Adobe Stock; 47 (LO), arsscreta/Getty Images; 48 (UP), Raul Garcia Herrera/Dreamstime; 48 (LO), Juan Carlos Munoz/Adobe Stock; 49 (UP), Victor Torres/Shutterstock; 49 (CTR), mardoz/Adobe Stock; 49 (LO), leelook/Adobe Stock; 50 (UP), Kent/Adobe Stock; 50 (LO), spiritofamerica/Adobe Stock; 51 (LE), Universal Images Group North America LLC/Alamy Stock Photo; 51 (RT), Ira Block/National Geographic Image Collection; 52 (UP), CHEN WS/Shutterstock; 52 (UP RT), dezign56/Shutterstock; 52 (LO), marekuliasz/Shutterstock; 53 (UP), (RT), Design Pics Inc/National Geographic Image

Collection; 53 (LO), Palo_ok/Shutterstock; 54 (UP), MarclSchauer/Shutterstock; 54 (jar on left), The Michael C. Rockefeller Memorial Collection, Gift of Mrs. Gertrud A. Mellon, 1969, 1978.412.231/Metropolitan Museum of Art; 54 (jar on right), Purchase, Rogers Fund and several members of The Chairman's Council Gifts, 2018, 2018.699/ Metropolitan Museum of Art; 55 (UP), Traveller70/Shutterstock; 55 (LO), Inge Johnsson/Alamy Stock Photo; 56, faraktinov/Adobe Stock; 57 (UP), New York Public Library/Science Source; 57 (RT), Robert Harding Picture Library/ National Geographic Image Collection; 58, Album/Alamy Stock Photo; 59 (clergy), Archivist/Alamy Stock Photo; 59 (lords & ladies), Ivy Close Images/Alamy Stock Photo; 59 (peasants), Chronicle/Alamy Stock Photo; 59 (LO), Science History Images/Alamy Stock Photo; 62, CPA Media Pte Ltd/Alamy Stock Photo; 63 (UP), Pelin/Adobe Stock; 63 (LO), Pictures from History/Bridgeman Images; 64 (UP background), natuliya/Adobe Stock; 64 (UP LE), S35ktmo/Dreamstime; 64 (UP RT), oliverfiction96/Adobe Stock; 64 (LO LE), B. David Cathell/Alamy Stock Photo; 64 (LO RT), Look and Learn/Bridgeman Images; 65, Gift of Etsuko O. Morris and John H. Morris Jr., in memory of Dr. Frederick M. Pedersen, 2001/Metropolitan Museum of Art; 66 (UP background), 3d-sparrow/Shutterstock; 66 (UP), Jayakumar/Shutterstock; 66 (LO), RealityImages/Shutterstock; 67, cascoly2/Adobe Stock; 68, CPA Media Pte Ltd/Alamy Stock Photo; 69 (UP), picturist/Adobe Stock; 69 (RT), Alisa/Adobe Stock; 70 (UP), ABCDstock/ Shutterstock; 70 (LE), CPA Media Pte Ltd/Alamy Stock Photo; 71, wealthy lady/Adobe Stock; 72 (cherry blossoms and firecrackers), asharkyu/Shutterstock; 72 (RT), ViewStock/Getty Images; 73 (UP LE), Peng Zheng/Dreamstime; 73 (UP RT), Volgi archive/Alamy Stock Photo; 73 (LO), Atman/Dreamstime; 76 (UP), Horváth Botond/Adobe Stock; 76 (LO), Philippe Clement/Shutterstock; 77 (UP), akg-images; 77 (RT), Mary Evans Picture Library; 78 (UP), Kharbine-Tapabor/Shutterstock; 78 (LO), Lunstream/Adobe Stock; 79 (UP), urika/Adobe Stock; 79 (LO LE), Alfredo Dagli Orti/Shutterstock; 79 (LO RT), De Luan/Alamy Stock Photo; 80-81 (background), Marian Weyo/Shutterstock; 80, SergeyKlopotov/Shutterstock; 81 (UP), Tony Cordoza/Alamy Stock Photo; 81 (LO LE), Harris Brisbane Dick Fund, 1932, 32.130.7a–l/Metropolitan Museum of Art; 81 (LO RT), Fletcher Fund, 1921, 21.139.2a–h/Metropolitan Museum of Art; 82, Look and Learn/Bridgeman Images; 83, Gianni Dagli Orti/Shutterstock; 84 (UP), Classic Image/Alamy Stock Photo; 84 (LO), Look and Learn/Bridgeman Images; 85 (UP), Anton_Ivanov/Shutterstock; 85 (LO), Giuseppe Rava. All Rights Reserved 2022/Bridgeman Images; 86 (UP), Production Perig/Shutterstock; 86 (LE), Serg Zastavkin/Adobe Stock; 86 (LO), alexat25/Adobe Stock; 87 (UP), tinnaporn/Adobe Stock; 87 (LE), PerfectLazybones/Adobe Stock; 87 (LO), irinabal18/Adobe Stock; 88-89, scaliger/Adobe Stock; 90 (UP), Claus Lunau/Science Source; 90 (LO), Lunstream/Adobe Stock; 91 (UP), Zim235/Dreamstime; 91 (LE), The Stapleton Collection/Bridgeman Images; 91 (RT), Kletr/Adobe Stock; 91 (LO), Look and Learn/Bridgeman Images; 92 (UP background), Gali Gali/Shutterstock; 93 (pomegranate), Taras/Adobe Stock; 93 (dates), denira/Adobe Stock; 93 (LO), DEA/G. Dagli Orti/Getty Images; 94 (UP), Archives Charmet/Bridgeman Images; 94 (LO), lobro/Adobe Stock; 95 (UP), keladawy/Getty Images; 95 (orange), zoomonpictures.it/Adobe Stock; 95 (coffee beans), Tetiana/ Adobe Stock; 95 (RT), Abdolhamid Ebrahimi/Getty Images; 95 (LO), mehmet/Adobe Stock; 96 (UP), Mohammad Barahouei/Dreamstime; 96 (LO LE), Valeriy Lebedev/Adobe Stock; 96 (LO), Pictures from History/Bridgeman Images; 97 (UP LE), Firas Nashed/Adobe Stock; 97 (UP RT), Everett Collection Inc/Alamy Stock Photo; 97 (CTR), Veneranda Biblioteca Ambrosiana/Mondadori Portfolio/Bridgeman Images; 97 (LO RT), Album/Alamy Stock Photo; 98 (UP), Lordprice Collection/Alamy Stock Photo; 98 (LO), Album/Alamy Stock Photo; 99 (UP), British Library/ Granger, NYC; 99 (RT), PjrWindows/Alamy Stock Photo; 100-101, M&N/Alamy Stock Photo; 100, kontrymphoto/ Shutterstock; 101 (UP LE), Pictorial Press Ltd/Alamy Stock Photo; 101 (UP RT), Mr Doomits/Adobe Stock; 101 (LO), Album/Alamy Stock Photo; 102, Franco Visintainer/Adobe Stock; 103 (RT), Cavan Images/Alamy Stock Photo; 103 (LO), Bridgeman Images; 104 (UP), Look and Learn/Bridgeman Images; 104 (LO), Pictures from History/ Bridgeman Images; 105 (RT), VTR/Alamy Stock Photo; 105 (LO), Oleksandr/Adobe Stock; 107 (UP), Granger, NYC; 107 (LO), Beibaoke1/Dreamstime; 108 (LE), CPA Media/Pictures from History/Granger, NYC; 108 (Murasaki Shikibu), coward_lion/Adobe Stock; 108 (RT), Art Collection 3/Alamy Stock Photo; 108 (Abu'l Qasim), Fabrizio Troiani/Alamy Stock Photo; 109 (UP LE), Bridgeman Images; 109 (UP RT), British Library Board/Bridgeman Images; 109 (Dante Alighieri), V. Korostyshevskiy/Adobe Stock; 109 (LO LE), GL Archive/Alamy Stock Photo; 109 (LO RT), National Museums Liverpool/Bridgeman Images; 109 (Giovanni Boccaccio), fabianodp/Adobe Stock; 111 (UP), Fototeca Gilardi/Bridgeman Images; 111 (LO), INTERFOTO/Alamy Stock Photo; 112 (UP), mitzo_bs/Adobe Stock; 112 (LO), Leonid Andronov/Adobe Stock; 113 (UP), Douglas Freer/Shutterstock; 113 (RT), Mega Pixel/Shutterstock; 113 (LO), Ironstuff/Dreamstime; 114 (UP), British Library Board/Bridgeman Images; 114 (LE), Olhastock/Shutterstock; 115 (UP), bzzup/Adobe Stock; 115 (LO LE), xpixel/Shutterstock; 115 (LO RT), Tatiana/Adobe stock; 117 (UP), Keith Heaton/Shutterstock; 117 (LO), Yuriy Kulik/Adobe Stock; 118 (UP), Chronicle/Alamy Stock Photo; 118 (LE), breakingthewalls/Adobe Stock; 118 (LO), Valentina R./Adobe Stock; 119 (UP), Bridgeman Images; 119 (RT), hotonewman/Adobe Stock; 119 (LO), North Wind Picture Archives/Alamy Stock Photo; 121 (UP), Heritage Image Partnership Ltd/Alamy Stock Photo; 121 (RT), The History Collection/Alamy Stock Photo; 121 (LE), Grafissimo/Getty Images; 121 (LO LE), Museum of London; 121 (LO CTR), Bridgeman Images; 122-123, JackF/Adobe Stock; 122 (UP), Smith Archive/Alamy Stock Photo; 122 (LO), Brooklyn Museum Costume Collection, 2009/Gift of Herman Delman, 1954/Metropolitan Museum of Art; 123, Album/Art Resource, NY; 124-125, Keith Corrigan/Alamy Stock Photo; 124, Phanie/Alamy Stock Photo; 125 (lice), Miramiska/Adobe Stock; 125 (UP), tusharkoley/Adobe Stock; 125 (RT), Sasajo/Adobe Stock; 126-127, ErreCh/Shutterstock; 126 (LE), Science History Images/Alamy Stock Photo; 126 (LO), Mary Evans Picture Library; 127, Heritage Image Partnership Ltd/Alamy Stock Photo; 128 (UP), Mazur Travel/Shutterstock; 128 (red resin), spline_x/Adobe Stock; 128 (licorice), Scisetti Alfio/Adobe Stock; 128 (LO LE), naskami/Shutterstock; 128 (CTR LO), tea maeklong/Shutterstock; 128 (LO RT), henk bogaard/Adobe Stock; 129 (UP), Svetoslav Radkov/Adobe Stock; 129 (CTR), Jonathan Nackstrand/Shutterstock; 129 (LO), Nitr/Adobe Stock; 130 (UP), British Library Board. All Rights Reserved/Bridgeman Images; 130 (LE), Celiafoto/Shutterstock; 131 (UP), Look and Learn/Bridgeman Images; 131 (LE), fotoearl/Shutterstock; 131 (RT), LaKirr/Shutterstock; 131 (LO), Bridgeman Images; 132, yblaz/Adobe Stock; 133 (UP), De Luan/Alamy Stock Photo; 133 (UP RT), Chris Hellier/Alamy Stock Photo; 133 (LO), Albert Knapp/Alamy Stock Photo; 134 (UP), National Museums Liverpool/Bridgeman Images; 134 (LO), 135 (LO RT), Bridgeman Images; 135 (UP), Science History Images/Alamy Stock Photo; 135 (LE), ZZTop1958/Shutterstock; 137 (UP), Lebrecht Music & Arts/Alamy Stock Photo; 137 (LE), The Stapleton Collection/Bridgeman Images; 137 (RT), Look and Learn/Bridgeman Images; 138-139, Oliver Gerhard/imageBROKER/age fotostock; 138, Scala/Art Resource, NY; 140 (UP), auris/Adobe Stock; 140 (LO), saiko3p/Adobe Stock; 141, Hao Zhou/Adobe Stock; 142 (UP background), Matorini/Dreamstime; 142 (UP), Christopher Scott/Alamy Stock Photo; 142 (LO), Heritage Image Partnership Ltd/Alamy Stock Photo; 143 (UP), Lennart/Adobe Stock; 143 (LO), Wood Ronsaville Harlin, Inc. USA/Bridgeman Images; 144, Alexstar/Adobe Stock; 145, swisshippo/Adobe Stock; 146 (UP), CCI/Bridgeman Images; 146 (LO), Sheldon Levis/Alamy Stock Photo; 147 (UP), arquiplay77/Adobe Stock; 147 (LE), Dmytro Surkov/Alamy Stock Photo; 147 (RT), trinurul/Adobe Stock; 147 (LO), fotomaster/Adobe stock; 148-149, Matorini/Dreamstime; 148 (UP), Granger, NYC; 148 (LE), Ingram; 148 (LO), verdateo/Adobe Stock; 149 (LE), Science & Society Picture Library/Getty Images; 149 (RT), Peter Ekin-Wood/Alamy Stock Photo; 150, Alexander Potapov/Adobe Stock; 151 (UP), Archivio J. Lange/NPL - DeA Picture Library/Bridgeman Images; 151 (LO LE), Lanmas/Alamy Stock Photo; 151 (LO RT), Serhiy Shullye/Adobe Stock; 152 (LE), grafikplusfoto/Adobe Stock; 152 (LO), javarman/Adobe Stock; 153 (UP), Lordprice Collection/Alamy Stock Photo; 153 (RT), Natika/Adobe Stock; 154-155, C. C. Wang Family, Gift of The Dillon Fund, 1973, 1973.120.4/Metropolitan Museum of Art; 154 (UP), Ylstock/Dreamstime; 154 (LE), Bridgeman Images; 155 (UP), Purchase, Miriam and Ira D. Wallach Philanthropic Fund Gift, 1991, 1991.74/Metropolitan Museum of Art; 155 (RT), Edward C. Moore Collection, Bequest of Edward C. Moore, 1891, 91.1.530/Metropolitan Museum of Art; 155 (CTR), SBS Eclectic Images/Alamy Stock Photo; 156 (UP), Look and Learn/Bridgeman Images; 156 (LO), The Picture Art Collection/Alamy Stock Photo; 157 (RT), Bridgeman Images; 157 (LO), Mary Evans Picture Library; 159 (UP), Bridgeman Images; 159 (CTR), Mary Evans Picture Library; 159 (LO), Francois Doisnel/Adobe Stock; 160 (LE), Veronica Louro/Shutterstock; 160 (RT), Juraj Lipták/Adobe Stock; 161 (UP), Max_grpo/Getty Images; 161 (jug), Shahin Mammadov/Adobe Stock; 161 (spoon), m_k_/Adobe Stock; 162, Science History Images/Alamy Stock Photo; 163 (UP LE), Photo 12/Alamy Stock Photo; 163 (UP RT), tarasov_vl/Adobe Stock; 163 (CTR), Romolo Tavani/Shutterstock; 163 (LO), The Maas Gallery, London/Bridgeman Images; 164, Morphart/Adobe Stock; 165 (UP), Bridgeman Images; 165 (LO), Art Collection 3/Alamy Stock Photo; 166 (UP), Bequest of Mrs. A. M. Minturn, 1890/Metropolitan Museum of Art; 166 (LO), Look and Learn/Bridgeman Images; 167 (UP), Artepics/Alamy Stock Photo; 167 (RT), Steve Estvanik/Dreamstime; 168-169, Science History Images/Alamy Stock Photo; 168, Prisma Archivo/Alamy Stock Photo; 169 (UP RT), baibaz/Adobe Stock; 169 (RT), Zuri Swimmer/Alamy Stock Photo; 172 (UP), North Wind Picture Archives/Alamy Stock Photo; 172 (LE), Beinecke Rare Book and Manuscript Library/Yale University Library; 173 (UP), IanDagnall Computing/Alamy Stock Photo; 173 (LO), JohanSwanepoel/Adobe Stock; 174, Bequest of George D. Pratt, 1935, 42.152.6/Metropolitan Museum of Art; 175 (UP), Lagui/Adobe Stock; 175 (LO), history_docu_photo/Alamy Stock Photo; 176 (UP), Peter Horree/Alamy Stock Photo; 176 (LO), Aleksandar Todorovic/Dreamstime; 177 (UP), Harper Collins Publishers/Shutterstock; 177 (LO), spiritofamerica/Adobe Stock; 178 (UP), Peter Brown; 178 (LO), krilerg/Adobe Stock; 179 (UP), The History Collection/Alamy Stock Photo; 179 (RT), Bridgeman Images; 180 (UP), Haver/Adobe Stock; 180 (LE), dudlajzov/Adobe Stock; 180 (LO), Crazy nook/Adobe Stock; 181 (UP), Bettmann/Getty Images; 181 (LE), Alessandro Cristiano/Adobe Stock; 181 (RT), jnsepeliova/Adobe Stock

CREDITS

Dedicated to all the teachers who inspired my love of history —MB

Copyright © 2023 National Geographic Partners, LLC. All rights reserved. Reproduction of the whole or any part of the contents without written permission from the publisher is prohibited.

NATIONAL GEOGRAPHIC and Yellow Border Design are trademarks of the National Geographic Society, used under license.

Since 1888, the National Geographic Society has funded more than 14,000 research, conservation, education, and storytelling projects around the world. National Geographic Partners distributes a portion of the funds it receives from your purchase to National Geographic Society to support programs including the conservation of animals and their habitats. To learn more, visit natgeo.com/info.

For more information, visit nationalgeographic.com, call 1-877-873-6846, or write to the following address:

National Geographic Partners, LLC
1145 17th Street NW
Washington, DC 20036-4688 U.S.A.

For librarians and teachers: nationalgeographic.com/books/librarians-and-educators

More for kids from National Geographic: natgeokids.com

National Geographic Kids magazine inspires children to explore their world with fun yet educational articles on animals, science, nature, and more. Using fresh storytelling and amazing photography, *Nat Geo Kids* shows kids ages 6 to 14 the fascinating truth about the world—and why they should care. natgeo.com/subscribe

For rights or permissions inquiries, please contact National Geographic Books Subsidiary Rights: bookrights@natgeo.com

Art directors: Eva Absher-Schantz and Dan Banks
Design: Project Design Company

The publisher would like to acknowledge the following people for making this book possible:

Michael Burgan, writer; Ariane Szu-Tu, editor; Jen Agresta, project editor; Sarah J. Mock, senior photo editor; Danny Meldung, photo editor; Gus Tello, designer; and Michelle Harris, fact-checker.

The publisher also thanks Peter Brown for his expert review of the manuscript, and Nicole Overton, Paul Cobb, and Ahmed Salim for their invaluable assistance with this book.

Library of Congress Cataloging-in-Publication Data

Names: Burgan, Michael, author.
Title: The Middle Ages / Michael Burgan.
Description: Washington, DC : National Geographic Partners, LLC, [2023] | Series: Weird but true! Know it all | Includes index. | Audience: Ages 8-12 | Audience: Grades 4-6
Identifiers: LCCN 2022024475 (print) | LCCN 2022024476 (ebook) | ISBN 9781426373299 (paperback) | ISBN 9781426373787 (library binding) | ISBN 9781426375491 (ebook)
Subjects: LCSH: Middle Ages--Miscellanea--Juvenile literature. | Civilization, Medieval--Miscellanea--Juvenile literature.
Classification: LCC D117 .B98 2023 (print) | LCC D117 (ebook) | DDC 909.07--dc23/eng/20220801
LC record available at https://lccn.loc.gov/2022024475
LC ebook record available at https://lccn.loc.gov/2022024476

Printed in South Korea
22/SPSK/1